The Complete Guide to
BUFFALO NICKELS
Second Edition

by
David W. Lange

DLRC Press

Books for collectors...

For Alba,

who helps me to keep this whole
coin thing in perspective

DLRC Press

Books for collectors...

Post Office Box 1061
Virginia Beach, Virginia 23451
(800) 776-0560 ❧ info@davidlawrence.com

www.davidlawrence.com

Printed in the United States

Acknowledgements

Among the people who figure prominently in this effort are Norm Talbert, Tom Miller, Bob Entlich, Leroy and Marilyn Van Allen, Bill Fivaz and J. T. Stanton. All have given freely of their specialized knowledge of error and variety coins.

The principal photography for this book was performed by Tom Mulvaney. His work includes the obverse and reverse photos of each date/mint combination, the error gallery and the grading guide. The enlarged variety photos were taken by Bill Fivaz, Ken Hill, Kimberly Levinson, J. T. Stanton, Tom Mulvaney and Leroy and Marilyn Van Allen. The photographs of the Smithsonian's pattern nickels were taken by Douglas A. Mudd of that institution. Permission to use the 1913-D (type 1) nickel on the cover of this book was provided by Bill Fivaz and the image comes to us courtesy of the American Numismatic Association.

The design and layout of this book is by John Feigenbaum of DLRC Press.

A special thanks goes to the following professionals who provided their insight with respect to rarity and/or grading, as well as offering other useful comments: Jack H. Beymer, Don Bonser, Walter Breen (deceased), Mark Feld, Timothy Hargis, Don Harris, Joe Hollingsworth, Ron Miller (deceased), Bob Patchin, Norm Talbert, Larry Whitlow and Phelps Dean Witter.

Others who provided reference materials used in the preparation of this book include Robert Van Ryzin, J. P. Martin, Craig A. Whitford, Cory Gillilland, Eric P. Newman, Mark Van Winkle, Andrew W. Pollock III, Harry Miller, Mrs. Frank L. Curnen, William R. Ayres, Jr., Joe Wargo, David Blasczak and David F. Cieniewicz.

Thanks go also to the following institutions that furnished historical photographs and/or information: National Archives, Washington, DC; Smithsonian Institution National Museum of American History, Washington, DC; South Dakota State Historical Society, Pierre, SD; National Cowboy Hall of Fame and Western Heritage Center, Oklahoma City, OK and the American Numismatic Association Library and Authentication Bureau, Colorado Springs, CO.

Foreword

by Bill Fivaz

I love Buffalo Nickels! And, because you're reading this, obviously you do too!

It's been called the "All-American Coin," a classic example of true Americana, and it is, along with the Lincoln Cent and the Mercury Dime, one of the most collected series in all of numismatics.

And well it should be, with James Earle Fraser's dynamic Indian profile on the obverse and a denizen of the West, a powerful bison, enhancing the reverse. Each design virtually fills its side of the coin, with the balance of the areas unencumbered by other features and with a minimum of wording. In short, it is a very attractive coin.

David W. Lange's superb presentation of the historical events leading up to the design and issuance of this coin is, by far, the most interesting and well researched of any I've read. Please do yourself a favor by reading the portion of this book leading up to the individual date-and-mint analysis, as it will give you a much better appreciation of this beautiful coin.

His date-and-mint analysis is offered in a very user-friendly format and is easily accessible. The photos of the individual coins, taken by the hobby's best photographer, Tom Mulvaney, provide the reader a wonderful example of the ultimate specimen for each issue, thereby presenting a challenge to assemble a world-class set.

The inclusion of a section on errors, as well as counterfeit and altered coins in the series, dovetails well with the many die varieties listed and illustrated under the appropriate date. Die varieties, incidentally, are fast becoming a very collectable segment of numismatics, and the Buffalo Nickel series is no exception. The recent discovery of two important overdates, the 1914/3-P and 1914/3-S issues, has given impetus to the search for other die aberrations, including "two-feather" varieties, "3-1/2 leg" issues and the possibility of a 1914/3 overdate from the Denver Mint.

The all-important subject of grading is well presented, and illustrations for each grade are included. The Estimated Rarity Rating by date and mint is an important segment of this book, too, as it provides the reader a path to follow in whatever grade he or she selects.

The bottom line is this: If you want a book that covers the subject of Buffalo Nickels as well as I feel it can be covered, you're holding it. Read it, use it and, most of all, enjoy it!

Author's Foreword

Special to the Second Edition

When the first edition of this book was published in 1992, it was my first attempt at such a vast project, and I approached it with some timidity. Unproven as I was, I didn't at the time realize just what potential existed within myself for research and discovery. Though I'd written many articles and columns on numismatic topics, the notion of writing and assembling an actual book remained quite challenging. Though I was pleased with the published product, and I've truly been gratified by the many nice comments it received from readers, a growing awareness came over me that this was less than a completed work. So many additional sources of information were uncovered during the first year after its publication that I immediately began thinking of a new edition.

As things turned out, this would have to wait some years. Almost as soon as the book reached print I committed myself to writing a similar work on Mercury Dimes that was published about a year later. That was followed by yet another book on Lincoln Cents, published in 1996. It was during preparation of that third title that my life underwent a dramatic transition. After nearly fifteen years in the engineering field, I accepted a position with Numismatic Guaranty Corporation as its director of numismatic research. In a classic example of the tail wagging the dog, my hobby was about to become my career. This entailed a move from my lifelong home of California to distant New Jersey.

It was a successful transition, though it did delay publication of my book on Lincoln Cents. Still, the move did not account entirely for the extraordinarily long time required to complete that book. There was a fundamental change in my vision of what the book should be. Perhaps it was my new role as a professional numismatist, but I now felt a far greater commitment to making the book a truly complete reference. I acquired copies of all the correspondence and documentation available from the National Archives pertaining to the creation of the Lincoln Cent, and I sat down to read. The wealth of information available precluded my settling for the superficial treatment of history found in most popular numismatic books. I decided to actually reprint much of this primary source material, fleshing out many of the characters who, previously, had been just names to me. This led to further research that included scanning page-by-page every issue of *The Numismatist* and *The Numismatic Scrapbook Magazine* from 1905 onward. The result of this tedious work was my inclusion of many anecdotes and bits of numismatic trivia that provided additional reading for even the most routine issues within the Lincoln series.

The Complete Guide to Lincoln Cents was written over a period of some two-and-a-half years, as compared with the six months required for the first edition of the present work and the eight months or so for my book on Mercury Dimes. It was an exhausting ordeal both for me and my original publisher, who ultimately decided that the finished work was more than he wanted to undertake. It was thus published under another company's banner, though it remained true to the established format for this series.

Nevertheless, I believe the difference in scope and scale between the Lincoln Cent book and its predecessors made it the best work I can do, and I have no regrets over the many lost weekends. The experience did, however, forestall the second edition of this present book, as I knew that I could not undertake the project with any less determination than I'd had when doing the Lincoln book. The first edition of *The Complete Guide to Buffalo Nickels* sold out several years ago, and there was sufficient demand to simply reprint it in the existing form. This would have been the smartest move from a business standpoint, and I must thank my publisher, John Feigenbaum, for permitting me the indulgence of rewriting the book almost in its entirety. It is a far finer work than the first edition, and I believe that all parties, especially the readers, will benefit from the extra effort lavished upon it.

David W. Lange
Morris Plains, New Jersey
June 21, 2000

Introduction

The late coin dealer Abe Kosoff, one of the most prominent figures in the coin business during the 1940s-60s, once conducted a survey of his customers and discovered that the Buffalo Nickel series topped the list as most popular. Several decades later these coins remain a favorite set to collect. While other series may enjoy the spotlight to a greater degree and have become the focus of investors and speculators, the Buffalo Nickel draws its continued popularity primarily from collectors.

The boldness of James Earle Fraser's designs and the uniquely American quality of the subjects portrayed have made it easily the most familiar obsolete United States coin to both numismatists and the general public. Although Buffalo Nickels have not been minted for more than 60 years, they still play a role in American culture, being used in the fashioning of Native American and Western style jewelry.

Countless other Buffalo Nickels have been reborn in a quite different form of folk art -- the so-called "hobo nickel." Almost from its inception, the nameless Indian's portrait has attracted would-be sculptors. Using the simplest of tools, these Michelangelos of the open road reshaped his profile into flappers and fools, soldiers and saints, bons vivants and bums. Among the latter were many self-portraits. When sold at a modest profit, these coins afforded the small necessities of a hobo's life. In recent years master engraver Ron Landis of the Gallery Mint has produced perhaps the most beautiful hobo nickels to date. These examples of the carver's art, both vintage and modern, are popularly collected by members of the Original Hobo Nickel Society. I am myself a member and, like all members, I've adopted a hobo name. Mine is "Frisco," a tribute to the place of my birth.

In addition to such "mutilated" nickels, thousands of these coins survive today as dateless relics of a fondly remembered past. No longer having numismatic value, such worn pieces stimulate the imagination of the collector, who can only speculate as to the desirable dates and mintmarks they once bore. That they continue to possess value as objects of art is a tribute to the genius of James Earle Fraser and to our rich American heritage.

With the supply of attractive and identifiable pieces limited, the value of these coins to the collector can only increase with the passage of time. Numerous scarce date and mint combinations have commanded premiums for decades, and the growth in the collecting of errors and varieties has likewise drawn these coins to the forefront.

Rarity aside, even the most common date Buffalo Nickel is a joy to behold in pristine mint condition. Fortunately, there are a number of dates for which such examples may be acquired at a reasonable cost. Whatever the collector's budget, he or she will find the collecting of this series an enriching experience. That this book may in some way contribute to such enjoyment is all that the author can ask.

Table of Contents

History of the Buffalo Nickel Series

A TIME FOR CHANGE

Beginning in 1907, a series of designs was introduced which would, over the next 15 years, completely transform the face of United States coinage. It was in that year that new eagles and double eagles bearing the masterful art of Augustus Saint-Gaudens were placed in circulation. America's pre-eminent sculptor, Saint-Gaudens had been commissioned by President Theodore Roosevelt to elevate the state of our coinage art to the levels attained by the ancient Greek coiners of the 5th Century, B.C.

Such an ambitious undertaking was rare in the history of the United States Mint. Previous coin designs had been prepared entirely within the insulated environment of the Mint establishment, with the result that practicality usually dominated aesthetic considerations. An enlightened leader, Roosevelt was determined to break this monopoly, and Saint-Gaudens would be his instrument of revolution.

Alas, the great sculptor died just as his golden masterworks were being prepared for circulation, and the further projects that had been envisioned were seemingly lost. Even so, as Roosevelt's term was ending in 1909, the movement he had conceived was serving as inspiration to others of like mind. The Lincoln Cent, introduced later that year, was a radical departure from the allegorical goddesses of previous United States coins,

Preliminary model by Fraser for the proposed new five cent piece
(William S. Nawrocki photo, Joseph Lepczyk/Craig A. Whitford Archive)

Inverse model of the adopted obverse dated 1912 and lacking the designer's initial F below date
(Nawrocki, Lepczyk/Whitford)

and this work was hailed by numismatists and the public alike.

Within the Treasury Department, some thought was given as to which coins could be redesigned. The Mint Act of September 26, 1890 prohibited the introduction of new designs for any denomination more often than once in 25 years. This meant that the only coins eligible for new designs were the five-cent piece and the silver dollar. As a curious aside, that law had specifically exempted from its provisions these very coins, as it was widely believed that both denominations then bore inferior designs that should be replaced immediately. As it stood, silver dollars hadn't been coined since 1904, and a resumption of striking didn't seem likely anytime soon. This left the five-cent piece as the focus of attention among interested parties.

That such interest existed is proved by a letter from prominent Philadelphia numismatist and coin dealer S. Hudson Chapman dated 1909 and addressed to Assistant Treasury Secretary Charles D. Norton. Chapman was serving as secretary to a committee chaired by fellow professional numismatist Thomas L. Elder:

> Our Committee feels that while at present the coins of our country are not what they should be artistically, and that while the new incuse types of gold coins are unsatisfactory,

inartistic and unsightly, that the recent agitation of this subject has brought about some reforms in the new St. Gaudens types and the Lincoln cent, which are in a degree encouraging. As the present nickel piece may now be changed without the act of law, that piece should be given especial attention. We believe that by keeping this matter constantly before the public and officials that a sentiment may be aroused which will result in legislative action and more artistic coins. We trust that President Taft may take as much interest in this matter as did Mr. Roosevelt, to whom great credit is due for his attention to the subject of our coinage.[1]

Inverse model of the adopted reverse
(Nawrocki, Lepczyk/Whitford)

The Mint's chief engraver, Charles Barber, began preparing models for a new nickel featuring a portrait of Washington. These were dated 1909 and 1910, and a few pattern strikes were made from the dies. It would be a feather in Barber's cap if Treasury Secretary Franklin Mac-Veagh were to select his design. The past three years had witnessed the introduction of no less than five new coins featuring the work of outside artists. Although none of the superseded designs had been Barber's, that of the current five-cent piece was his work -- the familiar Liberty Head Nickel of 1883.

Inverse model of the adopted obverse dated 1912 and bearing the initials JEF
(Nawrocki, Lepczyk/Whitford)

Numismatists knew that patterns were being prepared, but that didn't reduce their frustration at seeing no results. An editorial in *The Numismatist* for March of 1911 revived this crusade when it asked, "When are we going to have a new five-cent piece? Since 1892 [sic] the issue of a new five-cent piece has been lawful,

and each year we have been expecting the new design."

Evidently unaware of these developments, Eames MacVeagh, son of the treasury secretary, wrote to his father on May 4, 1911:

A little matter that seems to have been overlooked by all of you is the opportunity to beautify the design of the nickel or five cent piece during your administration, and it seems to me it would be a permanent souvenir of the most attractive sort. As perhaps you are aware, it is the only coin the design of which you can change during your administration, as I believe there is a law to the effect that the designs must not be changed oftener than every twenty years. I should think also it might be the coin of which the greatest numbers are in circulation.

The attached letter from Mr. Andrew explains the matter further and shows his interest in it, and I feel quite sure that the present director of the Mint would also be interested if he were stirred up about it. He is himself the possessor of a very rare and beautiful Greek coin.[2]

As the younger MacVeagh suggests, it was indeed Assistant Treasury Secretary A. Piatt Andrew who started the ball rolling on the new five-cent piece. As first conceived, however, the coin was to bear a Lincoln portrait. This was the idea of Mint Director George E. Roberts, though why he should want another such coin during the third year of Lincoln Cent production remains a mystery.

We know of the proposed Lincoln

Nickel through correspondence between Roberts and sculptor James Earle Fraser. It's not clear from these documents whether Fraser was commissioned by the director to prepare models or simply took the initiative himself, but his involvement in this project a full year before news of it reached the press suggests that he was sought by Roberts for his proven skill. In a letter dated June 13, 1911 Fraser responded to the director's desire for a Lincoln bust:

> I think your idea of the Lincoln head is a splendid one and I shall be very glad to make you some sketches as soon as possible and let you see them. I think they should be reduced to the actual size of the coin; otherwise we will not be really able to judge them, even in the sketch period. I will have that done here, where I can watch the process.[3]

Five weeks later, the work had progressed to the point where Fraser anticipated sending Roberts "some electro plates of the small sketches..." As had happened so many times before, the director was evidently being pressured by the Treasury Department to sponsor a design competition, this being perceived as the most fair means of obtaining new designs. Though such programs had proved disastrous in the past, the memory of government officials rarely extends beyond the current administration. Fraser voiced his skepticism of this policy in a letter to Director Roberts:

> In reference to competition, I think the great trouble is that you may have numbers of sketches in the competition one of which you choose and, if I'm not mistaken, you will be forced to stick very closely to that design, even though it might not be quite up to what you would want. Whereas, working with a competent man, there would be no doubt that a great many designs would be made; in fact, you would go on working till something of real merit was produced. You may say, if you like, that I would be perfectly willing to satisfy the Art Commission Mr. MacVeagh spoke of.[4]

Fraser's reference to the Federal Commission of Fine Arts suggests that the idea of a design competition may have originated there. Chartered by Congress in 1910 to oversee the aesthetic aspects of all federal building projects, its authority to evaluate coin designs was not made official until 1921. Nevertheless, its members maintained a keen interest in all matters relating to the arts.

An internal memorandum prepared by Director Roberts on March 18, 1913 reports that it was Secretary MacVeagh who, upon viewing Fraser's models, promoted the idea of a competition:

> The latter was pleased with the piece but cautious about committing himself to a change in the coin. He inclined to the opinion that if changes were to be made other artists should be invited to compete. The matter rested at this stage for some time and although there was more or less discussion over it, and interviews with artists and connoisseurs, it was nearly a year before the Secretary took up the subject seriously. By this time he had made up his mind that if any change was to be made he wanted the Fraser designs.[5]

By the time that MacVeagh had committed to the "Fraser designs," the proposed Lincoln Nickel had been replaced by the now familiar combination of a Native American bust and a bison figure. Fraser had himself suggested these motifs as being superior, and by the end of 1911 the Lincoln coin had been scrapped altogether. Sensitive to the director's wishes, Fraser had to proceed slowly with this notion, as is evident from his letter of September 19 to Franklin MacVeagh:

> Although I realize that no definite commission has been given me in regard to the designs for the new coins, I have become so much interested in the sketches that I have pushed them a little farther and now they are in the shape of electrotypes which I should like to submit for your consideration. Of course, this means that they are still merely sketches and not finished products, but I have had them reduced and made into their present form for the purpose of showing exactly what I would wish done, provided I finish them.
> At present, they are the size of the penny but they could easily be enlarged to any size desired. The idea of the Indian and the buf-

falo on the same coin is, without doubt, purely American and seems to me singularly appropriate to have on one of our national coins. You will see that the Indian is entirely different than any that has ever been used on a coin. Most of the heads have been Caucasians with an Indian head-dress; in this case, I have avoided using the war-bonnet and have made a purely Indian type.

Therefore, I should like to ask whether or not you would consider placing these designs on the nickel.

I have also carried the Lincoln head farther, not only because I was personally interested in it but because Mr. Roberts has rather encouraged the idea of my doing so.[6]

The numismatic community had since become aware that work was underway on a new five-cent piece, yet Editor of *The Numismatist* Edgar H. Adams was informed by Director Roberts that "no change in the design of the 5c nickel piece has been determined upon."[7] Indeed, little more was heard on the subject for some months. Finally, on January 13, 1912 Secretary MacVeagh confirmed his selection of Fraser as the designer of the new five-cent piece in a letter to Director Roberts:

I am now writing to Mr. J. W. [sic] Fraser in acknowledgment of the attached letter and apologizing for the fact that we have not heretofore been able to give the matter our careful consideration. I am also telling him that he may expect, within a day or two, to hear directly from you.

The sketches submitted by Mr. Fraser are in every way so satisfactory and he is a man who stands so high in his profession, that I am glad we all have agreed to let him continue with the matter without looking further or incurring additional delay. Will you, therefore, please write to him and tell him that the nickel five-cent piece is the coin for which we have been considering his designs and the only one that is available at this time. Tell him that of the three sketches which he submitted we would like to use the sketch of the head of the Indian and the sketch of the buffalo, subject to adaptation; the head of the Indian to appear on the obverse and the figure of the buffalo on the reverse. Only such inscriptions as the law requires should, of course, go on the coin, in order not to mar its beauty and to avoid crowding.

Please state to Mr. Fraser exactly what the requirements and restrictions of the law are in this respect, and ask him to submit a completed model and to state his price.[8]

The statutory inscriptions required on every United States coin include, in addition to the date and value, the following mottoes: IN GOD WE TRUST; LIBERTY; and E PLURIBUS UNUM. Given that Fraser's designs occupied nearly the entire fields of the coin, it would take some doing to incorporate all of this lettering. The artist expressed his anxiety in a letter to Director Roberts: "I believe in placing as little lettering as possible on the coin, since the design will be just so much better for the fewer things it contains. I am very anxious to go on with the designs and make them as perfect as possible, then have them reduced to the nickel size ..."[9]

The progress of the new five-cent piece stalled early in 1912, though Fraser himself seemed quite ready to proceed. Throughout this period Eames MacVeagh, who still maintained a strong interest in the new coin's development, penned a series of letter to Roberts and others in the Treasury Department inquiring about the delay in issuing the new nickel and Fraser's reaction to it. He received no satisfactory answer; at least, nothing survives within the Mint's correspondence that would account for the silence of February-May, 1912.

No more is known until June of that year, when Fraser wrote a letter to Roberts in which he seems a bit irritated:

The models for the five cent piece have been finished, and reduced in several heights of relief and therefore I am ready to come and explain, and have explained, to me, what is necessary, and to talk over some changes that I now think, since seeing the reductions, would prove advantageous.[10]

Fraser's letter suggests there may have been problems with the relief of his models. This is something that would have been noticed immediately by the Mint's chief engraver, Charles Barber. Since Barber was never pleased to have outsiders providing designs for United States coins, his manner could sometimes be quite abrupt. He was usually correct in matters relating to the practical side of coining, so he doubtless suggested changes for Fraser to make.

While this matter was pending, the Treasury Department made the mistake of prematurely announcing the new coin to the press in early July 1912. This prompted a flood of editorial comment on both the appropriateness of the new designs and the wisdom of making any changes to a coin so widely used. The usual number of crank letters was submitted to the newspapers' editorial pages, as well as to the Treasury Department itself. One of these stands out as more interesting than the others, if only because it elicited a reply from Secretary MacVeagh, to whom it was addressed:

> I notice in today's papers the anticipated change in the five cent piece and forthwith send my emphatic protest. It is quite enough to have the Indian on the one cent piece. As for the five dollar gold piece that is too, too bad! The Indian will never be forgotten. All children of every class sometime or other wear an Indian suit, mimic war dances and pow wows. If it is necessary to make a change could it not be as artistic as we have now!
>
> Please Mr. Secretary use your influence to have the Indian and the Buffalo placed somewhere else than upon our nice little five cent piece.
>
> Very Truly Yours,
> Elizabeth Holland Lake

MacVeagh's diplomatic response of July 12 says much about the motivation of the interested parties in creating a truly special coin:

> Your earnest appeal in behalf of the present 5c piece has been received. I quite agree with you that if we are to make a change the new piece should be at least as artistic as the old one but is this so very difficult? A coin to be artistic should be suggestive and in some sense characteristic of the country to which it belongs. That cannot be said of the present 5c piece. The Buffalo and the Indian are both peculiar to the United States, identified together with its past and worthy of such a memorial as an artistic coin would be. The merit of the idea would seem to depend upon the ability of the artist to give us something distinctive, pleasing and of

really national significance. Nothing has been determined upon but if such a result should be achieved we should count confidently upon your approval.[11]

Of course, the proposed new coin had its supporters, as well. Among these was Waldo C. Moore, a future president of the American Numismatic Association (1919-20) and most recently a member of the 1912 Assay Commission. Moore wrote to MacVeagh endorsing Fraser's radical departure for the humble nickel:

> In re- the new five-cent piece, I am aware that there is some opposition to the change, but never-the-less I am inclined to believe that a new five-cent coin with the American Buffalo on the one side and the American Indian on the other would be just the proper thing. Both the Buffalo and the Indian designs should be something artistic, nothing that would cause one to be ashamed. Let us have a coin so designed in commeration [sic] of the early Indian and Bison of North America.[12]

Seeking to deflect potential criticism of the new design, Secretary MacVeagh asked Fraser to have his work evaluated independently by several prominent figures within the art community, most of whom were also members of the Commission of Fine Arts. Among the respondents was Daniel Chester French, a sculptor whose works include the Minuteman statue reproduced on the Lexington-Concord Half Dollar and the seated figure of Lincoln within Washington, D.C.'s Lincoln Memorial. In his letter of July 17, French also makes reference to the abortive Lincoln coin project favored by Director Roberts:

> I have examined [the designs] carefully and with keen interest and I have no hesitation in giving them my hearty approval. They are very fine both in design and in execution and I think you have reason to take great satisfaction in the thought that this beautiful coin has been made by your direction and is to be struck during your administration. Mr. Fraser has my sincere congratulations on the result of his labors.
>
> Mr. Fraser has also shown me the design containing the head of Lincoln and I cannot help expressing the hope that this may be utilized for one of the other coins. It would seem

a pity to lose so charming an example of the medallic art and so striking a portrait of the man.[13]

Further praise was heaped upon Fraser's designs by artist Edwin Howland Blashfield, who likewise couldn't resist reminding the secretary about the Lincoln head, possibly at Fraser's urging:

> I saw Mr. Fraser's designs yesterday and greatly approved of them.
> I like the Indian and am delighted with the Bison which would give us, it seems to me, a distinctively national American coin. Our national Eagle is a superbly decorative bird and should always remain on some of our coins, but we share him with Germany, Russia, Austria and other states. The Bison is all ours.
> I wish that Mr. Fraser's profile Lincoln could be used some way. It seems to me fine in the rather high relief treatment which he has accorded to it and the silver is handsome in its color-effects of surface.[14]

An additional endorsement was received from Cass Gilbert, a member of the Commission of Fine Arts and a celebrated architect whose Woolworth Building was just then reaching completion in New York City. Gilbert added to his approval of the designs his desire "that the coin could be struck with the deeper relief which Mr. Fraser has shown in some of the models he brought with him..." He then qualified his statement with the notation "he tells me that some practical objections are raised by your department."[15] The need to strike up a coin fully with just a single blow of the press was a concept alien to most medallists, who were accustomed to taking multiple impressions from the dies while the planchet was carefully annealed between blows. As Gilbert suggested in his letter to MacVeagh, Fraser seems to have reconciled himself to this restriction with far less fuss than other artists commissioned by the U. S. Mint.

In fact, on the surface things were going quite well. As the Commission of Fine Arts was not then in session, several of its members had given their individual approvals to Fraser's designs, and both the Mint and the Treasury Department were in favor of making the change. In fact, so eager was MacVeagh to see the new coin in production that he wrote to Director Roberts on August 30 urging him not to delay in proceeding. "If I were you I would not wait any longer," MacVeagh stated. "It is evident that we can have the complete approval of the Fine Arts Commission."[16]

A FLY IN THE OINTMENT

Just when it seemed that all was set to prepare final models and then reduce these to hubs the Mint became involved in a protracted and troublesome debate with the manufacturers of coin-operated vending machines. The press release of July 1912 announcing that a revised five-cent piece was in the offing alarmed these businessmen to such a degree that they managed to delay introduction of the new nickel by several months, fearing that the new coins would not operate their machines.

While their concerns ultimately proved to be without foundation, the cause for their anxiety was understandable. The five-cent piece was perhaps the most widely used coin of that time, as there were endless articles and services it could procure. To emphasize its importance in the mechanical vending industry, one alarmed businessman even submitted a list of the various items and entertainments then available through vending machines. While some of these remain familiar today, albeit at much higher prices, it's interesting to note those that have passed into history: savings bank saving stamps; Biograph instruments; gas meters; counterfeit coin detectors; soda fountain checks; sheet music; and celluloid collars.

Aggravating the situation further was an ill-conceived and especially ill-timed bill recently passed by the House of Representatives. This called for the coining of a three-cent piece, a denomination retired in 1889 but now deemed necessary once again due to inflation. What especially concerned the manufactures and users of coin-operated machines was that various proposals were being floated for revising both the dimensions and compositions of the one-cent and five-cent pieces so as to conform to the new three-cent coin. There was talk of aluminum-brass alloys and perforated planchets, all of which agitated the vending machine industry far beyond what would have been the case if only a simple redesign of the existing nickel was at stake. While the Senate wisely voted down this bill, the debate over it during 1911-12 left the vending machine industry in a defensive state of mind. When the announcement was made in July of 1912 that a new nickel was being prepared, it was widely misinterpreted that this change would include revised dimensions and/or composition.

Although both Roberts and MacVeagh received numerous letters from various manufacturers and users of coin-operated machines from the summer of 1912 through the winter of 1913, certainly the most persistent of these correspondents was a Mr. Clarence W. Hobbs, president of the Hobbs Manufacturing Company of Worcester, Massachusetts. The Hobbs Company, whose principal product was "Paper Box Machinery," also marketed a coin-detecting device that discriminated between genuine coins and slugs. Writing on behalf of his own firm and also as treasurer of the American Stamp and Ticket Vending Machine Co., his primary customer, Hobbs would continue to pressure the Mint over the new nickel even after the coins were in circulation. Fearing that the discrimination mechanism of his machines would not function properly with the new nickels, he caused delay after delay as he first sought to dissuade the Mint from issuing a new coin and then, after conceding that the new design was inevitable, nitpicked Fraser and Roberts ceaselessly over its relief and mechanical properties.

While Hobbs was always courteous and respectful in his letters to the director and secretary, he remained insistent that the new coins be designed so as to fit his machines, rather than his machines being retrofitted to accept the coins. The obvious absurdity of this was clear to James Earle Fraser. When pressed by Director Roberts to adjust his models to be in conformance with the requirements of Hobbs and other manufacturers, Fraser vented his frustration, as in this letter from August of 1912:

> If you wish me to do so I will leave Monday night for Worcester to see about the coin detecting machine and show them the new design.
>
> I can't go before on account of press of work. It seems to me, that as the coins are changed only once every twenty years new detectors could be made in accordance.
>
> In Europe, I believe, when a new coin comes out the old ones are called in within the space of two years. Is that right?[17]

While the battle with Hobbs went on, it was believed prudent to show the models for the new nickel to President William H. Taft, though by law his approval was not required. This was merely a courtesy, as the treasury secretary had the final say on all matters of coin design. MacVeagh reported to Roberts September 14 on his meeting with Taft at the executive office in Beverly, Massachusetts:

> I visited the President on Thursday and showed him the letters of Messrs. Blashfield, Gilbert and French; and told him what was going on. He told me he did not know anything about it before; and I think he felt as though I had not wished to appeal to his artistic sense. He asked me if I had the "things" along; but of course I did not have them. He was extremely nice about it; and the interview of course left me free to go ahead; and he expects nothing further.
>
> It occurred to me, however, after I left Beverly that it would be a polite thing to have Mr. Fraser go to Beverly and show the designs to the President; and if possible to have Mr. French go with him - Mr. French being in the neighborhood.[18]

An appointment was made for Fraser to show the models to the president on October 5 at the executive office in Beverly, which served as Taft's little White House. When it turned out that the president had to leave Beverly that same day, Fraser was wired in advance that the meeting was therefore postponed. The artist inquired a week or so later as to when he would have his audience with the president, but there was no answer immediately forthcoming. It was not until October 24 that Secretary MacVeagh wrote to the president's office expressing concern that work on the nickel was being held up pending the president's approval. He received a curt reply that "Mr. Forster (the president's secretary) wired department that the President had been consulted and had no interest in seeing Mr. Fraser."[19]

Evidently, with Taft just two weeks away from his re-election bid, he had more urgent matters on his mind. While this must have come as a blow to those interested in the new nickel, it did remove one more obstacle by firmly eliminating the president from the approval process. This left only the obstinate Mr. Hobbs. Still firing off letter after letter to MacVeagh, Roberts and Fraser stating his mechanical requirements for the new nickel, he was a constant thorn in their sides.

Any hope that the coin would be ready in time for the new year was dashed when the two opposing parties failed to reach a compromise. Fraser went so far as to furnish Hobbs with electrotype shells of his models for testing and modification. The changes demanded by Hobbs were unthinkable to Fraser, who had carefully worked out the proper balance and scale of his models over the course of a year. His stance that the Hobbs Company was in a better position to modify its machine than he was to modify his designs was received with sympathy by Roberts, who nevertheless wanted the artist to make as many of the requested changes as he could without impairing the ultimate work.

A letter from Hobbs to Fraser dated November 22 is typical of the many received and will suffice to explain his grievances with the new coin:

> I am returning to you today by Registered Post the two proof coins which you entrusted to me for measurement. In our study of these in connection with the current five-cent coin, and the coin testing machines, we find that there will be needed no change in design of the Buffalo side but only a slight change in proportion - or size.
>
> The absolute requirements are:
> (1)   A root circle inside the rim on the reverse
> (2)   A root circle inside the rim on the face which in this connection is the Buffalo
> (3)   A broken circle inside the inscription
> (4)   A bearing on the face (body) of the figure
> (5)   A center bearing
>
> With the proof coins I am sending to you a standard five-cent coin marked with the circles indicated, 1, 2, and 3; also the center point, 5. Herewith I hand you a drawing which gives the diameters and heights upon which we must rely to successfully test the old and the proposed new coins, and to separate from them foreign, false, and imitation coins and tokens.
>
> The design of the Buffalo and the Indian head are so excellent that it would be asking too much to have them changed, but the results desired can all be achieved by reducing the Buffalo figure 8/100 of an inch in length and otherwise in proportion. This will give ample space for the outside circle, and the broken circle will then fall just outside the hump. The height between the root circle 2, and the circular bearing 4 and the center point 5 are easily accomplished without in any way altering the general design. The foundation for the feet could be lowered a trifle and the root circle 2 pass over it without altering the design. It is nearly low enough now.
>
> There should also be a root circular bearing around the Indian head inside the rim, as shown upon the reverse of the marked coin. This is for the purpose of getting the standard thickness upon which the test measurements are based.
>
> The bottom of the broken circle 3 need not be flat, but may be more or less so, provided we have approximately the root depth at all points.
>
> With the slight changes indicated I cannot see that the appearance of the coin will be marred and the public will then be given the full advantage of the automatic sales devices which I described to you.[20]

The effect of all this mind-numbing engineering detail on a sensitive artist such as James Earle Fraser can easily be imagined. Venting his frustration with Mr. Hobbs, Fraser wrote to Director Roberts on December 1:

I notice that there is no concession whatsoever on his part; he asks me to reduce the size of the buffalo, inscription, etc., eight-one-hundredths of an inch which, practically is one-tenth of an inch. I have carefully considered every space surrounding the buffalo and have changed them all back and forth many times, arriving at this design only after the utmost care. So you see how radical any change approximating one-tenth of an inch would be in the relation of the spacing in a coin of this size.

Not only that but it is no sure thing that the coin-detector will be a practical success. I suggested that the first rim of the nickel be used instead of the circle inside the fretwork and also to bring the second circle nearer the stars. This I am sure can be done.

It is plain to be seen that they are trying to get everything they can at my expense; and I hardly think that the Government should be forced to accept a design which is inferior to the present one when the machine could be changed without altering to any great degree its effectiveness, thus leaving the coin nearly in its present state. There would have to be a slight reduction even in event of using the first rim of the nickel. In the future, this would eliminate the wide rim which, on the present coin, is wholly out of proportion to its size thereby adding to the difficulty in making the design. We should think of the future, also, so that it will not be possible to have this trouble again. I called on Mr. French and he thinks it would be nearly out of the question to make so great a change in my design.

I only received the coins from Mr. Hobbs last Saturday so have had little time to work on them. I am perfectly willing to anything to help them without making the design bad.

As I understand it now, I am to make the reductions, send them to the Mint and see what the result will be. I will have Mr. [Henry] Weil send you the price on the reductions; it may be cheaper than usual as this is a trial.[21]

Sensing that the situation was at an impasse, Secretary MacVeagh urged Roberts to give Fraser final approval for the existing models. Fraser responded December 11, "I would like to leave New York for Washington on the coming Monday night to show you what it is necessary to do with the new nickel."[22]

As evidence that the work was nearing completion, a letter was submitted the following day to Director Roberts by Henry Weil of Medallic Art Company in New York. He quoted a figure of $100 per side for the obverse and reverse hub reductions. It's interesting to note that Fraser sought to have this work done outside the Mint's own engraving department, as there were precedents for this. Henry Hering, assistant to Augustus Saint-Gaudens designs and the actual sculptor of the famed ten- and twenty-dollar gold pieces bearing Saint-Gaudens' designs, complained bitterly in 1907 that Charles Barber was unable to make proper reductions using the Mint's own Janvier reducing lathe. Two years later, Victor D. Brenner had likewise submitted hub reductions of his Lincoln Cent models prepared by Mr. Weil.

Weil's quote proved acceptable, and the requisite hubs were ordered December 18.[23] While it's not specifically stated in surviving documents, it may be assumed that these were then forwarded to the Philadelphia Mint's engraving department where dies were sunk from them under the supervision of Charles Barber. Superintendent John H. Landis wrote to Director Roberts on the final day of 1912 advising him that "Mr. Fraser has expressed a desire to be present at the experimental striking of the new five-cent piece," adding that "we will be ready for this trial on Tuesday morning, January 7th." In fact, the bill from Medallic Art Company for "2 steel hubs for the new nickel from models by J. E. Fraser" bears this same date, though an internal memo prepared two months later by George Roberts gave the date of first coining as January 6.[24]

It's evident that the first strikes were satisfactory to those witnessing their production. Indeed, so confident was Superintendent Landis of the test dies' usefulness that he was able to furnish Director Roberts with this glowing report:

In reply to your letter of the 10th instant, in reference to the new 5-cent piece, I beg to inform you that the Engraver states that he intends to harden the hubs today and will be ready to begin the manufacture of the working dies on Monday. If he stops all other work he can have a supply of dies sufficient to start all the presses in this mint and also ship to the

Denver and San Francisco mints in ten days after receipt of your order. The Superintendent of the Coining Department states he can turn out $15,000 per day if all the presses are put on this coin.[25]

Ever the spoiler, Chief Engraver Barber couldn't resist sounding a lone sour note on the proceedings:

> It may not have occurred to you the necessity of having possession of all models and moulds of whatever kind or condition, also bronze castings or wax reductions, in fact everything that has been made in connection with the new Five Cent coin.
>
> I wish to call your attention to this matter because from the character of the design and execution of the same I am convinced that it would be an easy matter to counterfeit the new coin and therefore, it is most desirable that everything that has been made in the production of the same should be deposited in the Mint.[26]

Barber's reference to the flawed execution of Fraser's design was prompted by the distinctive irregularity of the coin's surfaces. Rather than creating conventional, smooth fields Fraser had given them the rough-hewn texture that was then in vogue among sculptors. This same style of modeling was utilized a few years later by sculptors Hermon MacNeil and Adolph Weinman in preparing new designs for United States coins, and in each instance Barber exacted his revenge and artistic predilection by smoothing out the fields shortly after production had begun.

While Barber was grumbling to himself, Director Roberts was faced with a far more serious problem. The ever-attentive Mr. Hobbs had only stepped up his challenges to the new coin now that it was a reality. Writing to Roberts from New York City on January 20, Hobbs took the liberty of repeating his stated position for what must have seemed like the hundredth time:

> As Mr. Fraser has probably informed you, we, by acting on your suggestion of working together, have come to the conclusion that certain modifications can be made in the new five cent coin which will make it possible it [sic] to be used on our machines and at the same time not detract from its artistic value.
>
> Mr. Fraser has sent the modified dies to Philadelphia today and our inventor, Mr. George Reith, will be in Philadelphia tomorrow morning to go over the matter very carefully with the die makers. I therefore sent you a telegram asking you to be kind enough to wire authority to the Philadelphia Mint to take this matter up with Mr. Reith.
>
> We greatly appreciate the attitude of yourself and Mr. Fraser in this matter for it was a question of the most serious import to us. Our machines are now in daily use in the Hudson Tunnels and will soon be in many other important places in this City and Boston.[27]

Both MacVeagh and Roberts, aware of their sensitive positions as political appointees, did not wish to dismiss these claims, and Fraser was again called upon to make refinements to his models. Indeed, another invoice is found from Medallic Art Company dated January 20 for "2 steel hubs, new nickel, final models by J. E. Fraser $200.00." The inclusion of the word "final" is most instructive as regards the attitude of everyone involved with the project. Fraser himself summed it up neatly in a telegram to Director Roberts that same day in which he reported "The dies are finished and will be in Philadelphia tomorrow, delay caused by working with inventor until he was satisfied, the coin is practically the same."[28]

It seems that there may have indeed been some flaw in Fraser's original models, as revealed in a letter from Superintendent Landis to Director Roberts:

> As requested in your telegram of today [January 21] and your conversation over the telephone, I beg to enclose herewith one of the new 5-cent nickel pieces struck today from the dies as modified by the Engraver. The only change is the border, which has been made round and true. The model was all free hand work and therefore not mechanically correct, which it had to be in order to conform to the requirements of modern coinage. The change was approved by Mr. Fraser this morning and he expressed himself as highly pleased, considering we had improved the piece.[29]

Amazingly, the director received yet

another letter from Hobbs three days later: "I am quite disturbed this morning at the report which he [Reith] brings back that the changes which were promised by Mr. Fraser have not been made in the dies, and that one hundred sets of dies of a pattern which practically precludes us from using the coin in our machine, have been prepared ready for use."[30]

Fraser wrote to Roberts on the 26th expressing his belief that nothing further would be gained from continued modifications to his models:

> I don't know whether you understood that the first models were carefully worked over to fit the coin-detecting machine and in making the second dies, I tried to have them absolutely correct. But, as we have seen, the difference after the reduction was made was so slight that my two-weeks work went for nothing.
>
> The Hobbs people have offered to pay me for my time but I am not sure if that would be proper or the right ethics. You understand that the designs were finished six months ago, to our satisfaction and to the satisfaction of the Art Commission; so that all the work done since then has been at the instigation of the Hobbs Manufacturing Company. I could have done several medals in the time I have spent in changing the design to the one-thousandth-part of an inch, back and forth, innumerable times.

In the same letter, Fraser informed the director of his satisfaction with the dies prepared by Charles Barber: "I find the engraving which was necessary to make the two sides of the coin fit exactly, the reduction of the edge and the simplifying of the background under the Buffalo's head beautifully done, showing no difference between the surface which I put on the models and the one they have made." He summed things up by stating, "I am delighted with their work at the Mint."[31]

Two days later, Fraser again wrote to Director Roberts complaining of Mr. Hobbs' persistent demands for further modifications. These now seemed to be completely irrational, as George Reith, the Hobbs Company's own engineer, had approved the revised coin:

> Mr. Reith distinctly said to Mr. Barber, Mr. Hensen (his own partner), and myself that it would make no difference, that it was alright to go ahead with the coining and that he could arrange his dies to suit the coins and could do so without any doubt. Mr. Hensen said "Are you sure" and he said "I am sure." He said he would make a flexible die like the one he made to fit the one cent piece. I asked him how that worked and he said it worked perfectly.[32]

Charles Barber verified Fraser's account of the trial strikings of January 28, but also cautioned that Mr. Henson had warned him George Reith was apt to be "over sanguine." Barber reported further that Hobbs was still not satisfied with the coin as it then stood and was requesting further modifications. Fraser, however, considered the matter closed. In a letter to Secretary MacVeagh the following day, the artist made it clear that he would make no further changes to his models.

He followed this with another letter on February 8 that ran to ten typewritten pages. In it he chronicled the entire frustrating history of the Indian Head/Buffalo Nickel. He also reminded the secretary that he (MacVeagh) had given his approval to the models December 18, 1912. In summation, Fraser stated that, "I have complied with the demands of the Hobbs Manufacturing Co. on every occasion, except the last, and this I cannot comply with because I am sure that it would result in destroying the artistic value of the original design which you have approved."[33]

Eames MacVeagh, the secretary's son who had been a keen observer of the proceeding from the outset, wired his father on February 10:

> Awfully sorry to learn of the opposition to the new nickel. Hope you will be able to put it through, no matter what compromise may be necessary as I feel anything would be better than the old one and that the bending [sic] machine may not be permanently effective against counterfeits.[34]

Director Roberts wrote to Secretary MacVeagh on February 10 expressing continued concern over the impasse between Fraser and Hobbs. He believed that however frustrating Mr. Hobbs' criticisms were they should not be dismissed: "The importance of the automatic vending machine has grown upon me during the negotiations and I think the question of whether it shall be ignored or not should be decided now upon broad grounds of public policy . . ." In an alarming note, he added that with respect to Fraser, "we can better pay him and throw his work away than adopt it if to do so is contrary to sound public policy."[35]

"YOU WILL PLEASE, THEREFORE, PROCEED WITH THE COINAGE OF THE NEW NICKEL."

Seeking to bring the matter to a conclusion, Director Roberts held a meeting February 14 that was attended by all interested parties. Present were Roberts; Charles Barber; Messrs. Hobbs and Carpenter of the Hobbs Manufacturing Company and their attorneys; Messrs. McKenney and Pritchard; George Reith; Mr. Henson, representing both Reith and his co-inventor of the coin-detecting machine; James Earle Fraser and his attorney, Meredith Hare. In the course of this meeting it was revealed that of the dozens of companies making coin-operated machines, only Mr. Hobbs' firm and its principal customer, American Stamp and Ticket Vending Machine Co. (Astumco), continued to insist on changes to the new nickel.

MacVeagh advised in a letter to Roberts that, "the commercial interests involved in this case are not relatively important." He went on to say, "If we should stop new coinage -- which is always allowed every twenty-five years -- for any commercial obstacles less than imperative we should have to abandon a worthy coinage altogether. This would be a most serious handicap to the art of the Nation; for scarcely any form of art is more influential than an artistic coin, where the coin is widely circulated." The secretary concluded his letter with the flat statement, "You will please, therefore, proceed with the coinage of the new nickel."[36]

This, in fact, was done. The first Indian Head/Buffalo Nickels coined for circulation were struck on February 17, and the coins were released March 4. MacVeagh's assessment of the Hobbs Company's impact on the vending machine industry was born out following an investigation by Fraser's attorney, Meredith Hare. Curious about the grand pronouncements Hobbs was making about his coin-detecting machine's widespread usage in the Northeast, Hare challenged Hobbs' claim that the Hudson River tunnels authority had expressed great satisfaction with it. Hare then wrote the following to Secretary MacVeagh on February 19:

> To-day I have had an interview with Mr. Wilbur Fiske, the executive officer of the Hudson & Manhattan R. R. Co., who has charge of such matters, and he showed me a copy of a letter he had sent to the agent of the Hobbs Manufacturing Co. telling him that the Hudson & Manhattan R. R. Co. was entirely dissatisfied with the coin-detecting machine and required him to have them all removed from the railroad's premises.[37]

Hare emphasized that the letter he was shown was dated February 10, four days before the meeting at which Mr. Hobbs had once again sung the praises of his machine and proclaimed its widespread acceptance. The attorney did not yet know that MacVeagh had already ordered mass production of the new nickels, and his concern was understandable. After all the delays prompted by Hobbs and his agents, the entire episode had proved to be a complete waste of time.

Still insistent that his objections to the coin had been prematurely dismissed, Hobbs actually wrote to President Taft with his sad story. When the president's secretary, C. D. Hilles, forwarded this letter to MacVeagh asking for an explanation, the latter was clearly angered. He informed Hilles of his repeated indulgences of Hobbs, adding that, "In return for this, Hobbs sends these delectable communications to the President."[38]

MacVeagh had clearly washed his hands of the entire matter. For Fraser, however, this was still not the end. There remained the matter of his fee, as well as payment to Henry Weil of Medallic Art Company for the hub reductions. An exchange of letters passed between Director Roberts and the artist debating the exact point at which Fraser's services were concluded and how much of his time and work should be compensated by the Mint. The bill he submitted also included the cost of several trips made to Washington and Philadelphia over the long course of the coin's development. Fraser was particularly emphatic how much of his time had been lost in the Hobbs affair, time that he'd devoted at the specific request of the director and the secretary. Embarrassed by this confrontation with the facts, Roberts had no choice but to approve the voucher submitted by Fraser, and the latter was finally paid for his year's work on March 3, 1913. Weil's payment was received shortly thereafter.

As noted previously, the new nickels went into mass production at the Philadelphia Mint February 17. Dies were immediately shipped to the other mints at Denver and San Francisco, where coinage commenced within a week. The coins went into general distribution March 4. Ever since the Mint's press release of July 1912, requests had been coming in from banks for the new nickels. There was evidently some confusion regarding the new issue, as the early inquiries refer to a coin featuring "a buffalo and a figure of Liberty." By the time the coins were in actual production this mistake had been sorted out. The following letter to George Roberts from John R. Washburn, assistant cashier of the Continental and Commercial National Bank of Chicago, is typical:

On January 16th we wrote you relative to the securing of $2,000 in the new design of nickels, and you informed us that the amount could be obtained about February 15th.

Judging by the orders we are receiving from our various correspondents the amount for which we originally asked will be insufficient, and we would inquire if the amount of coin issued will permit of our securing $5,000 of them.[39]

When they did make their appearance the coins were a hit with seemingly everyone. Among the fortunate few to receive a sneak preview were the members of The American Scenic and Historic Preservation Society. Writing to Director Roberts on February 26, Society President George F. Kunz reported on the popularity of the new coins:

THE NICKEL 5c PIECES were one of the features of the Indian Memorial, and no one more than the President, myself, and our Indian guests, could feel greater appreciation, nor express more marked approval of these novel and beautiful products of the Mint, than were felt and expressed when the bag of coins was opened and the pieces distributed.

I wonder if it is possible to have either 100 or 200 more of them? The Art people are so much pleased with them that they want more. Two of the coins went to the new art exhibition, and two were placed on exhibition in the American Numismatic Society.[40]

The new nickel was not universally praised, however. Edgar H. Adams, editor of *The Numismatist*, had this to say:

It is to be regretted that the new coin does not show much more finished die work, which could easily have been accomplished. We are inclined to think that the rough finish of the design will encourage counterfeiters, whose handicraft need not now fear comparison which it has met in the past with the ordinarily delicate and finished mint issues. The new piece certainly has radically changed the old-time tradition that Columbia is our best representation of "liberty."[41]

Prior to 1923, when it was transferred to the Smithsonian Institution, the U. S. Mint's own cabinet of coins was displayed at the Philadelphia Mint. Seeking to update this collection, the acting superintendent reminded Director Roberts that, "When here, you verbally authorized me to place specimens of the different varieties of the new five-cent nickel piece in the Cabinet. Can I have two specimens of the first variety and two of the large diameter variety struck and placed in the Cabinet, or will you supply them from those sent to the Bureau?"[42] This was evidently done, as the Smithsonian now holds two examples each of the trial strikings (see page 26).

Also seeking to enhance the Mint's cabinet was its curator, Dr. T. L. Comparette. Writing to Roberts on March 13, Comparette argued his case for obtaining Fraser's original models:

> Could we secure the original models of the new Five-cent piece? It is hard to see why they should remain in the possession of the artist; and if obtainable I should be delighted to have them for exhibition in the wall case. The original models would please many who now criticise [sic] the coins, because the inscriptions would be more distinct and the types better adapted to the field in the large model than on the coin. If we could not get the plaster model then we cartainly [sic] should have the bronze replica from which the die-sinker made the hub -- lest he make some more hubs.[43]

Fraser did indeed send Comparette the bronze models, or galvanos, of the Indian Head/Buffalo Nickel. However, the artist must have retained his intermediate models, as many of these turned up in his estate and are now in private hands. More about remaining examples of Fraser's work may be found within his biography starting on page 24.

AN UNFINISHED WORK

Dr. Comparette's allusion to problems with the inscriptions on the new nickel was valid. Though Fraser had resisted including the statutory inscriptions required on all United States coins, he met with just limited success. While LIBERTY fits in nicely, the legend E PLURIBUS UNUM was painfully crowded and not entirely legible. Mint Director Samuel Moore had wisely removed this Latin text from several U. S. coins during the 1830s, as he understood it to be redundant with the inscription UNITED STATES OF AMERICA. His successor, George Roberts, would have done well to follow this example, but he evidently felt restrained by law. For reasons unknown, the motto IN GOD WE TRUST was left off the nickel, yet nothing survives in the way of published protests over this omission.

Among the few persons sounding a sour note with respect to Fraser's nickel was Edgar H. Adams, editor of *The Numismatist*. In the May 1913 issue he took exception to many of the coin's features:

> The prediction of numismatical experts that the lead-like appearance of the new nickel, because of the rough surfaces, would make easy the counterfeiting of it, is already being fulfilled. From Philadelphia comes the report that the slot machines in that city are being flooded with counterfeits. As the danger of getting bogus coins increases, popular objection to the new nickel will be still more pronounced, and may become so strong as to force, before the year ends, some alteration in the design that will make it to conform more satisfactorily with what is of practical necessity in the case of a piece of money of so wide a circulation as the nickel. Satisfactory changes in the design might be as follows: Retain the head of the Cheyenne Indian, which is really an artistic creation, but reduce the size so as to give more field surface to the obverse. Above the head place the word "Liberty" and, underneath, the date in figures as large as those of the old design. If the initial of the designer's name is retained, let it be incused in the bottom of the Indian's neck. Eliminate the buffalo from the reverse entirely. Discard also the motto, "E Pluribus Unum," as there seems to be no good reason why it should appear on any of our coins. Around the upper border place the legend "United States of America;" in the center the figure 5, as appeared on the old shield nickels; and, on the lower border, the word "Cents." Give the field on both the obverse and reverse a smooth, level surface. A design of this kind would be sufficiently artistic, while there could be no objection to it from a practical point of view.

Fortunately, Mr. Adams' radical changes were not effected, as these would have rendered the coin just another Victorian entry in the tradition of Barber and Morgan. While the coins otherwise met with almost unanimous praise, their introduction to commerce quickly revealed another design problem that had eluded even the nitpicky Mr. Hobbs. It was evident from just the slightest amount of wear that the coin's denomination FIVE CENTS would be reduced to invisibility in only a few years' time. While the design was distinctive enough to preclude any doubt as to the coin's face value, the

Mint was overly sensitive on this point, remembering the fiasco of 1883.

The Liberty Head Nickel, introduced that year, had featured a large Roman numeral V as its sole indication of value. Capitalizing on the nickel's similarity in size to the gold half eagle, a few opportunists plated these coins and passed them as five-dollar pieces before the design became familiar. Addition of the word CENTS to subsequent issues of this type solved the problem, but the lesson learned from that experience persisted in the collective memory of Mint officers, and a solution was sought which would prevent a recurrence.

This situation was brought to the attention of James Earle Fraser, who responded to Director Roberts on April 1, 1913:

> I have your letter in reference to the five cent piece. Other sized letters can be made and I am ready to try them, but it strikes me that the five cents on the new nickel although it is small can be seen clearly and its meaning to a foreigner is much clearer than "one dime" on the ten cent piece and the "V cents" on the old nickel.
>
> A coin is known by its <u>design</u> and when it is well known it is never questioned even when the inscription is entirely worn away. Not one person in ten thousand reads the inscription on a coin before paying it out. However if you wish it I will come to Washington and we can decide on what is to be done.[44]

Chief Engraver Barber strengthened the denomination on one working die by hand and struck an example for comparison with the regular pieces. He then advised Director Roberts that "If you think well of the alteration we could hold up the coinage for a short time while I made a new hub which would not take more than ten days, when we could go on with the coinage. As the demand for this coin appears to have abated I think it would cause no inconvenience."[45]

The director was still anxious over the possibility of the new coins being gold plated, so he instructed Barber to have several examples gilded to test the ease with which it could be done and the similarity in appearance to a coin comprised of .900 fine gold. The engraver reported his progress on April 24:

> I have just returned from the gilder who does our work whenever needed and find it is quite possible to copy the color 9/10 fine gold, but the gilder explains that the difference in the surface and design would make 9/10 fine shade differently and therefore, it would be necessary to experiment with different solutions to find which fineness would best give the color of our gold coinage, all of which can be done by any gilder, but would involve expense.
>
> I enclose a five cent nickel coin which I think is very close to the 9/10 color, which was done while I waited by using an old solution.[46]

Fraser approved Barber's strengthening of the words FIVE CENTS, but he refrained from any additional involvement with the project. He informed Director Roberts of this in a letter dated April 25 in which he clearly understood that this was to be the only change made. Evidently the director was still concerned about the coin's value wearing away, as he authorized Barber to make a more radical change. Barber further modified the reverse hub by placing the words FIVE CENTS within an exergue cut into the grassy plain. While protecting the denomination from excessive wear, this change also diminished to some degree the boldness of Fraser's original rendition.

Seizing this opportunity and further succumbing to his own artistic prejudices, Barber opted to smooth out the roughened fields that characterized the original models. Fraser had intentionally used this treatment, as it was in vogue among medallists at the time. In fact, the artist had previously praised the Mint for successfully transferring its distinctive quality to the finished coins. What his thoughts were upon seeing the modified, or Type 2, Buffalo Nickel does not appear in surviving correspondence.

We can place the timing of this transition from the original edition, or Type 1 Buffalo Nickel, to the revised Type 2 from Barber's letter to Philadelphia Mint Superintendent John H. Landis dated May 6. In it Barber reveals, "I have made the desired change in the Five Cent coin and submit a piece for final approval. If it is satisfactory I can make coining dies at once. If the Director will wire or phone us as soon as he approves the change it will save time and facilitate our resuming coinage."[47]

A curious letter survives dated May 23 in which the assistant treasury secretary advises Director Roberts that, "The change suggested by Superintendent [Frank] Leach of the San Francisco Mint in the lettering of the obverse side of the nickels, especially in the word "Liberty", is approved." Since no change was evident in the obverse inscriptions before the introduction of a new master hub in 1916, it's obvious that this action was never effected until that time. Still, it reveals a deficiency in the coin's lettering that was evidently aggravated by using the dies so long that erosion caused these peripheral features to become distorted. In an important letter from Barber to Roberts written a few weeks after the transition to Type 2 nickels, the engraver addressed these concerns:

> The change suggested can of course be made, whether the life of the die will be increased "fifty per cent" is a correct statement is very doubtful, and only a trial will demonstrate.
>
> It is an open question whether the life of the die is as important a matter as the quality of the coin and I quite agree with you that the dies are run too long and more dies should be used.
>
> There must always be a first and a last point of the die to give out and the question is, which is the more important, if the inscriptions remain good and the Indian head and buffalo are worn smooth it cannot be claimed as an improvement.
>
> The fact is the design is too large for the size of the coin and no thought has been taken of the necessary inscriptions. The coin has the appearance of having been made with the sole object of covering the whole space with an indian head on one side and a buffalo on the other, the inscriptions being an after thought.
>
> To make the changes it will be necessary to reduce the relief of the shoulder of the indian as the date rests upon the shoulder, to increase the depth of the date without reducing the shoulder would make matters worse instead of better, it would surely require more pressure

to get a perfect impression of the die and that would make the life of the die shorter instead of longer.

> We now find that the date is the last place the metal fills and therefore to simply make the date deeper you will readily see would not be an improvement without as said before reducing the relief of the shoulder.
>
> Mr. Clark has just handed me the following which does not bear out the statement that the change already made will make "longer the life of the dies."
>
> Last 12 pairs of dies before change, average per pair 150,168, 12 pairs since change, average per pair 109,389.[48]

Barber's assessment that the only way to protect the date from wear would have been to reduce the relief of the shoulder was absolutely correct. Something like what was done with the value FIVE CENTS would have been necessary to protect this critical feature, yet in the end no action was taken. Roberts believed that further changes would draw too much public notice. The folly of this oversight became apparent within a few years, but it was too late to save millions of nickels from eventual obscurity. How different would be the collecting of these coins if every piece remained identifiable!

THE END OF THE TRAIL

As the novelty of the Buffalo Nickel wore off, so did the documentary trail. Very little in the way of mint records or correspondence survives to tell the story of this series after 1913. Perhaps more would be available today if not for an outrageous act on the part of a former mint director. Responding to President Jimmy Carter's general call for a reduction in government waste, his mint director, Stella Hackel, took the initiative of destroying all of the mint records that had not yet been transferred to the National Archives. This comprised nearly the entire record of the U. S. Mint's activities for the 20th Century. What may have once existed regarding the Buffalo Nickel and other contemporary coinage has been seemingly lost forever.

This crime is compounded by the fact that the *Annual Report of the Director of the Mint,* once an absolute treasure chest of useful numismatic information, began to decline in both scope and scale after 1920. The editions up to that time do contain some interesting nuggets, such as the average number of strikes per die at each of the mints, but later volumes contain little information relating directly to the coins themselves.

In the absence of published information, the coins must tell their own story. Much can be inferred by examining the various issues through the end of the series in 1938, but the separating of fact from speculation will always remain a challenge to numismatists. One of the clearest interpretations that can be made is that economy gradually overtook quality as a priority at the United States Mints. Charles Barber had already expressed his concern over this in his 1913 letter to Mint Director George Roberts in which he stated, "It is an open question whether the life of the die is as important a matter as the quality of the coin and I quite agree with you that the dies are run too long and more dies should be used." Indeed, the attractiveness of the Buffalo Nickel would at times be overshadowed by poor quality examples struck with inadequate contact from overworked dies. This is particularly true of nickels coined at the Denver and San Francisco Mints from 1917 through 1926. Some of the scarcest dates are made more so by having been indistinct from their inception. Nickels with much of their original luster still evident yet having only the detail of a low-grade coin are plentiful from this period.

Other information regarding specific date/mint issues will be found in Chapter 6. Therein, each coin in the series is examined in detail, and whatever is known regarding the circumstances of its production is included.

When its 25-year minimum life span had been reached, the Buffalo Nickel was unceremoniously discarded in favor of the current design featuring President Jefferson and his home, Monticello. This decision had already been anticipated within the Treasury Department, which announced its plan as early as January 25, 1938.[49] While the new coins were not released until November, supplies of the existing design were sufficient to preclude striking Buffalo Nickels anywhere other than the Denver Mint that year. A large percentage of the 1938-D Buffaloes were hoarded in uncirculated condition, making such coins far more common than worn examples.

The old nickels remained in circulation in ever diminishing numbers through the mid-1960s. The occasional odd piece found after that time was almost certain to be dateless. With the growing demand for such coins in jewelry manufacture, even these are no longer seen. The Buffalo Nickel has become just a memory for most, but its place among collectors is already secure.

RETURN OF THE BUFFALO NICKEL?

A sentimental favorite, the Buffalo Nickel has been the subject of several short-lived letter-writing campaigns that sought to supplant the upstart Jefferson type. These efforts were all doomed, as the bold relief of Fraser's models is simply too intimidating to the current establishment of the United States Mint. The demand for billions of coins annually requires that each working die be able to produce a million strikes or more, something not possible with a high-relief issue.

But while the Buffalo Nickel is not likely to be seen in circulation again, there is an alternative possibility. Since 1995, Senator Ben Nighthorse Campbell (R-CO) has attempted to revive the Buffalo Nickel in the form of a silver commemorative issue. This non-circulating coin would be struck to the traditional coin silver standard of .900 fine and sold at a premium to collectors. When first introduced that year, his bill called for the striking of not more than one million pieces per year for each of the years 1998 through 2000.[50]

Senator Campbell's campaign began

Postcard distributed in 1993 to promote Senator
Campbell's Buffalo Nickel campaign
(Mitchell Simon)

when he became aware that national parks in his home state of Colorado and throughout much of the nation were suffering from a lack of federal funding. Both necessary maintenance and desired improvements were suffering, and he sought to alleviate at least some of the shortfall through a commemorative coin campaign. His bill to have silver editions of the Buffalo Nickel dated 1998 through 2000 was introduced in several successive Congresses, only to languish each time.

On March 8, 2000 Senator Campbell introduced a new version of the bill (S. 2217) calling for the issuance of a one-year-only silver dollar using the Buffalo Nickel design.[51] On April 12, Congressman Frank Lucas (R-OK) introduced in the House a companion bill (H.R. 4259) that reads very much like Campbell's Senate bill. Both call for the coining of up to 500,000 pieces. In each bill the profits from a ten-dollar per coin surcharge would go toward the National Museum of the American Indian in Washington, DC, a part of the Smithsonian Institution.[52]

As this book goes to press, it remains unknown whether either legislator will be successful in his respective program. One thing is fairly certain, however. Should this coin type be reproduced in either the size of a nickel or that of a silver dollar, the relatively high relief of the Buffalo Nickel and the great amount of field that both the Indian portrait and the bison figure occupy will probably be modified by the U. S. Mint. Both conditions are radically at odds with current coin production, which demands low relief and generous free space around the devices. A new version of Fraser's bold design will be about as true to the original as the American Eagle bullion coins are to their antecedents by Adolph Weinman and Augustus Saint-Gaudens.

James Earle Fraser had made numerous studies of Native Americans before undertaking the task of creating an Indian head for the nickel. His most famous work, aside from the coin, is his sculpture "The End of the Trail." This work depicts an Indian hunter astride his horse, both figures bowed in a expression of weariness and despair. Although its first modeling pre-dates the nickel, this work in its final form was one of the highlights of the 1915 Panama-Pacific International Exposition in San Francisco. Its powerful character clearly demonstrates that Fraser possessed a rare grasp of the subject matter and was a master at rendering figures in relief.

The obverse of the Indian Head/Buffalo Nickel portrays a mature warrior facing right. His hair is braided in the style of the plains Indians with a ribbon securing the braid. Two feathers are affixed near the part in his hair, and a third one is only partly visible. The garment across his shoulder provides a foundation for the coin's date, and Fraser's initial letter 'F' appears below the date. Completing the obverse is the legend LIBERTY following the curve of the rim at the two o'clock position. On both the original model and the struck coin, the subject appears to be in a contemplative state with eyes half closed.

The coin's reverse is dominated by a left-facing full figure of an adult male bison. It

Iron Tail, an Oglala Sioux, photographed by Delancey Gill in 1913
(Smithsonian Institution, print courtesy South Dakota State Historical Society)

stands at rest upon a grassy mound bearing the value FIVE CENTS. Below the denomination is the mintmark letter 'D' or 'S' for branch mint coins, while those struck at the Philadelphia Mint bear no mintmark. UNITED STATES OF AMERICA appears in an arc above the bison, each word separated by tiny dots. Lastly, the legend E PLURIBUS UNUM is crowded into three small lines above the bison's rump. Clearly, the coin would have benefited from the omission of this last feature required by law.

An immediate question that arose following the introduction of the new nickel was the identity of the obverse model. Such was the interest shown by both numismatists and the general public alike that Fraser eventually felt compelled to respond in some way. Pressed for an answer, he revealed the names of Iron Tail, a Sioux, and Two Moons, a Cheyenne, as being among the three models engaged. His memory failed him on the identity of the third, leading to generations of speculation and opportunism for those with an interest in the matter.

Starting in the 1920s and lasting for up to fifty years, a handful of Native Americans earned a meager living on the basis of their claim to being the Indian on the nickel. In appearances at county fairs, store openings and the like, these claimants usually omitted any reference to the previously named models and were invariably introduced as being over 100

Two Moons, a Cheyenne
(National Archives)

Adoeette, or Big Tree, a member of the Kiowa
(NA)

years of age. The likelihood of any native who posed for Fraser still being alive after the passage of more than 80 years is slim, yet even today such stories may appear in the general press.

The most reliable evidence suggests that the third model was Big Tree, a Kiowa. That this Indian did indeed model for James Fraser at some time prior to 1912 was later confirmed by the artist's wife and fellow sculptor, Laura Gardin Fraser. She also named Iron Tail as her husband's favorite subject of the many studied.[53] Indeed, Iron Tail bears a remarkable resemblance to Fraser's bust and clearly possessed the strongest claim to being the Indian on the nickel. That he was the primary model for this portrait is verified further in a 1915 letter to Director Roberts from Dudley P. Lewis:

In October 1914 you kindly wrote me a letter relative to my inquiry as to the information I had received relative to the Indian's portrait on the famous "Buffalo Nickel." You said "I

have always assumed that the Indian head on the new nickel was simply the artist's ideal of the Indian type." Shortly after I received a similar letter from former Treasurer Lee McClung, Yale Class of 1892. Later I met the sculptor James E. Fraser - MacDougal Alley, New York. I told him that if he used the face of "Chief Iron Tail" as reported - I wanted to include that fact with the enclosed account of my Yale Class Dinner . . . Mr. Fraser said "In making that portrait the face of the magnificent old Indian, Chief Iron Tail, was uppermost in my mind."

Lewis enclosed a full-length profile photograph of Iron Tail taken in May of 1914. Now held by the National Archives, this photo is in an envelope clearly marked "Photograph of Chief Iron Tail whose profile appears on the Buffalo nickel."[54] Even so, the Indian Head must still be considered a composite rather than a portrait, as Fraser's archives reveal countless photographs and drawings of Native Americans, most done years earlier. His own statements to the effect that the Indian profile

In profile, Iron Tail clearly possessed the strongest claim to being *the* Indian on the nickel
(Gill, SI)

is merely representative of a type are also a matter of record.

One of the more amusing stories to arise from the controversy surrounding the model's identity was published in *The Numismatist* for January of 1935. It began with a wire service news story:

> Mae West has wired Secretary of the Treasury Morgenthau at Washington asking him to help her to find some young descendant of the American Indian who posed for the original on our buffalo nickel. She wants to have the handsomest descendant of this handsome brave appear with her in the early sequences of her next film, "Now I'm a Lady," in which Mae plays a cowgirl on a ranch near an Indian reservation. Mae was informed the Indian she sought probably would turn up on a Montana reservation, so we asked the studio traffic manager to find out cost and time required to make the trip there. "I want to see my Indian in person," she smiled, "and see if we would go all right together in my picture."

Responding to this story was Charles F. O'Malley, district secretary of the American Numismatic Association for New Jersey. On September 28, 1934 he wrote to Mae West to inform her of the model's identity:

> There is considerable controversy as to what Indian actually did pose for the coin. Some authorities claim that the figure is a composite of several Indians. Chief Iron Tail, of the Sioux Tribe, lays claim to being the model from which James Earl [sic] Fraser designed the coin. Iron Tail for a number of years traveled with that Wild West (no pun intended) Show, known as the 101 Ranch.
>
> Another claimant of the honor is John Two Moons, the son of Tsh-Sha-A-Nish-Is or Two Moons, who was engaged in the Custer massacre. Having known Chief Iron Tail personally, I am inclined to credit his claim.
>
> Do not let the word "Chief" confuse you, as anyone who has a beaded vest and an old pair of mocassins is called "chief" these days.
>
> So much for the redskins. Why not rewrite the script and change the character to a 260-pound Irishman. I might apply for the job myself.

Much to his delight, O'Malley received a characteristically sarcastic reply from Mae West who observed, "Yours is a good idea -- pure and simple. Well, anyway, simple." Ultimately, the part was played by actor Tito Coral who, it was

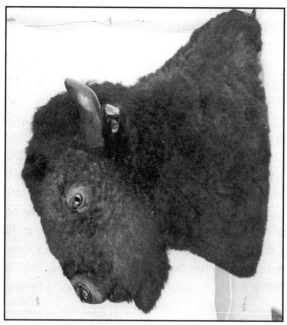

The mounted head of Black Diamond still exists
(Mrs. Frank L. Curnen)

noted, "looked like the Indian on the current nickel coin."[55]

The reverse of Fraser's five-cent piece is no less memorable in its profile view of a bison bull. In recalling this particular work, Fraser spoke of its unique character: "My first objective was to produce a coin which was truly American, and that could not be confused with the currency of any other country. I made sure, therefore, to use none of the attributes that other nations had used in the past. And, in my search for symbols, I found no motif within the boundaries of the United States so distinctive as the American buffalo."[56]

From the above quotation, it would

The author photographed with the head of Black Diamond in 1993
(Mrs. Frank L. Curnen)

appear that even the artist preferred the familiar term "buffalo" to the more zoologically correct bison. Semantics aside, the model for the nickel's reverse is known to have been a bull named Black Diamond. This animal was then a resident of New York City's Central Park Zoo and was already about seventeen years old at the time. Fraser's own correspondence reveals his exasperation in attempting to keep this beast posed in profile as depicted on the coin. Evidently quite uncooperative, it insisted on confronting the artist head on and would return to this stance immediately after being corrected.[57]

Black Diamond has occasionally been cited as the model for the $10 United States

James Earle Fraser's adopted models for the Indian Head/Buffalo Nickel,
photographed at the Philadelphia Mint Engraving Department.
(Bill Fivaz)

Note of 1901, the so-called "buffalo bill." This attribution is incorrect, as the greenback actually portrays Pablo, a star attraction at the National Zoo in Washington, D.C. This mistaken identity is understandable, as the $10 note was in use alongside the nickel through the late 1920s.

Nearly twenty years old in 1915, Black Diamond was soon declared too elderly to stay on at the zoo and was auctioned that summer in a sale of surplus livestock. The bison went for $300 to a poultry and game dealer by the name of August Silz who had it slaughtered on November 17, 1915. The animal weighed 1,550 pounds at the time of its death, and from this was obtained 750 pounds of dressed meat.[58] The meat was offered at $2 per pound as Black Diamond Steaks,[59] while the head was mounted by Fred Santer of New York City, who also fashioned a 13-foot square automobile blanket from the buffalo's hide.[60] Black Diamond's mounted head hung on the wall of Mr. Silz's meat company at 414 West 14th Street in New York City for decades afterward. Around 1927 Silz sold his business to his former employee, Benjamin H. Mayer, and Mayer's partner, Morris Hoffman. Black Diamond was included in the sale provided that the trophy would remain on display. This it did until Hoffman & Mayer, Inc. closed in 1977, whereupon the head was relocated to the home of Mayer's daughter, Marjorie Mayer Curnen.[61] It remains there to this day and has proved to be something of a local tourist attraction. It is especially popular with visiting groups of school children. Black Diamond further served as a drawing card to the 1985 convention of the American Numismatic Association in Baltimore, where the mounted head was displayed within the bourse room.

James Earle Fraser

The future creator of the Buffalo Nickel was born in Winona, Minnesota in 1876. Raised on the northern prairies of the Midwest, he was a witness to the sorrowful plight of both the Native American and the bison.

Fraser displayed a precocious talent for fashioning three-dimensional figures from materials at hand and was accepted as a student at the Art Institute of Chicago when not yet sixteen. His first major work was destined to remain his best known, despite a lifetime of achievement. Fraser completed "The End of the Trail" while still in his teens, a feat which attracted the attention of the art community and earned

James Earle Fraser, circa 1912
(National Cowboy Hall of Fame & Western Heritage Center)

him an invitation to study at the *Ecole des Beaux Arts* in Paris.

After a memorable five years in the City of Light, Fraser returned to America and continued his studies under the guidance of Augustus Saint-Gaudens, who was hailed as the most brilliant sculptor of his age. In turn, Saint-Gaudens considered Fraser his most gifted pupil. During this period Fraser completed numerous portrait busts and other works, in addition to teaching at the Art Students' League in New York City from 1906-11.

The opportunity to create a circulating coin memorializing both the American Indian and the bison was a commission Fraser took to heart. Driven to near extinction just fifteen years earlier, the bison still existed in a total population of little more than one thousand animals. While this number grew rapidly after 1913, Fraser and his contemporaries feared the loss of such a uniquely American symbol.

In the same year that the Buffalo Nickel entered circulation Fraser married Laura Gardin, a fellow artist of renown and the future sculptor of several commemorative half dollars and numerous medals. In the forty years that followed, until his death in 1953, Fraser completed dozens of commissioned works in a variety of sculptural forms. He returned to the familiar themes of the Native American and the bison only rarely. His Theodore Roosevelt Memorial at the American Museum of Natural History in New York City included the full figure of an Indian chief.[62] A smaller work titled "Buffalo Herd" was completed in 1950. Cast in bronze, it depicts a stampede of adult bison and calves.[63] Perhaps the most intriguing work from his later years was a revised obverse bust for the Lincoln Cent. Dated 1952, Fraser created it in anticipation that changes would be made to the cent in 1959 on the sesquicentennial of Lincoln's birth. He was correct in that respect, though it was the coin's reverse that was ultimately changed.[64]

James Earle Fraser left behind a rich legacy of both completed and proposed works. Many examples of his preliminary work in plaster have survived. Perhaps the finest collection of these resides within the National Cowboy Hall of Fame and Western Heritage Center in Oklahoma City. Originally part of the collection that both Frasers maintained in their Westport, Connecticut studio, these items were willed to Syracuse University in New York following the death of Laura Gardin Fraser in 1966. The Oklahoma City museum purchased the artworks for its collection, though the Frasers' personal papers remained with the university.

In 1981, some thirty lots of the Frasers' plaster models, including several for the Buffalo Nickel, were auctioned by Joseph Lepczyk in Lansing, Michigan. In speaking with the assistant curator of the National Cowboy Hall of Fame, Lepczyk learned that numerous shattered works had been left behind at the Westport studio as junk, but evidently some intact works had been overlooked. Exactly how these were obtained was never established, but no one stepped forth to challenge their sale or the right of the new owners to hold them. As the most desirable pieces, the Buffalo Nickel models brought prices ranging from $1900 to $4100.[65] Now widely dispersed, these only rarely appear on the market and may be expected to bring somewhat higher prices.

The first impressions of the Indian Head/Buffalo Nickel dies were taken on January 7, 1913. Although the test was judged successful, no record exists of what became of these prototype coins. It may be assumed that they were destroyed. The first trial strikings to be announced occurred six days later. Some seventeen pieces were coined of the regular design with the normal flat-top 3 in the date but lacking Fraser's initial 'F.'[66] These were mechanically conventional in all respects and had a diameter of 21.3 mm, nearly the same as the Liberty Head Nickel of 1883-1912. Of the original number coined, two have been preserved in the Smithsonian Institution's National Numismatic Collection and are illustrated here. Six of the remaining pieces were reportedly destroyed and the rest distributed to the artist and various officials.[67]

One week later, nine pieces were coined of the regular design as adopted. This outcome of this test was reported by Philadelphia Mint Superintendent John H. Landis to Mint Director George Roberts:

I beg to report that on Tuesday, January 21st, forty nickel blanks were procured from the Superintendent of the Coining Department, nine of which were struck from the dies of the new design 5-cent nickel piece in the presence of Messrs. Barber, Norris, Hart, Mr. Fraser, the designer, and two representatives of the automatic vending machine. One of these pieces was forwarded to you and eight are in the possession of the Engraver. The remaining thirty-one blanks have been returned to the Superintendent of the Coining Department.[68]

Five were reportedly destroyed, leaving four examples which, unless pedigreed to this particular emission, would be indistinguishable from ordinary Type 1 nickels.[69] Since no documentation survives linking any known coins to the event, these must be considered untraceable.

Work continued on perfecting the dies and, as revealed by a January 22 letter from Superintendent Landis to Director Roberts, even the planchets were subject to experimentation:

Today, in the presence of Messrs. Clark, Buckley, Bird, Hewitt, Proud and myself 60 milled nickel blanks, in three lots of 20 each of different cutting and milling, were used in experimental strikes with a view of ascertaining the most suitable blank for the new design five cent nickel piece. After these experiments had been completed the 60 pieces were destroyed in the presence of Mr. Clark and myself.[70]

Two days later the tests continued, with Landis again reporting to Roberts: "I beg to inform you that in further experimental work in connection with the new design 5-cent nickel piece thirteen (13) pieces were this day struck in the presence of Messrs. Clark, Buckley, Bird, Hewitt, Proud, and myself. These thirteen pieces were immediately thereafter destroyed in the presence of Mr. Clark and myself."[71]

When it appeared that all was in readiness for mass production, the unceasing protests of Mr. Hobbs again interfered. In an attempt to satisfy him, a test of the existing dies was performed for George Reith, the co-inventor of the Hobbs detecting machine, and a Mr. Henson, who was evidently Hobbs' business agent. An account of this trial was prepared for Superintendent Landis by Chief Engraver Charles Barber:

Mr. Reith came by my office first and explained what was required to make the coin acceptable to the Vending Company. Mr. Henson, also a representative of the Company, came next and Mr. Fraser last. The subject was fully discussed in all its bearings. Mr. Fraser was more than satisfied with the hubs as made by me, and disapproved of the new reductions from his altered model. As Mr. Reith could not judge from the hubs whether a coin made from the dies would be satisfactory to him and suitable to his device, I proposed that a coin should be struck in the presence of these three gentlemen. This suggestion was gladly accepted. The regular blanks were procured and the first pair of finished dies that my hand rested upon in the die drawer was taken. We then proceeded to the medal room, and, in the presence of the three gentlemen mentioned, Mr. Hart, foreman of the medal room, struck the coins as I suggested -- that is, one piece would be struck and then measurements would be made by Mr. Reith; then another piece would be struck and the same process would be gone through; this was done until nine pieces had been struck and measured by Mr. Reith. I proceeded in this manner, to give Mr. Reith full opportunity to see what difference there was likely to occur in different pieces arising from different degrees of malleability. I found Mr. Reith had provided himself with a micrometer gauge with adjustable points, making a most delicate instrument, as it allowed him to measure the smallest points of the coin. He was given every opportunity to satisfy himself that the coins were all that he needed or desired for the device he was making. He was given his own time, not hurried, or influenced in the least. After deliberating and measuring in every way he desired, he expressed himself as entirely satisfied.[72]

Notwithstanding the assurances of George Reith that all was well, Mr. Hobbs remained obstinate. In response to his ongoing charge that the bust was too close to the border for proper recognition by his machines, the Mint prepared a collar that was slightly greater than normal in diameter (22.1 mm). The idea was to simulate the effect of proportionally reducing the Indian's head without actually performing this tedious and time-consuming task.[73] On February 13, a number of trials were made with dies of this second prototype. Like the coins struck one month earlier, these pieces lacked the designer's initial. In contrast, however, they bore a round-top 3 in the date, narrower borders and a noticeably sharper LIBERTY. Of four such examples coined, the two illustrated here remain in the National Numismatic Collection, another was given to some unrecorded Mint official and the fourth was reportedly destroyed.[74]

The production coin that ultimately resulted from these experiments was a compromise, having the flat-top 3 and shallow LIB-

ERTY of the first prototype and the narrower border of the second. Of the trial strikings not destroyed or held permanently by the Smithsonian Institution, a few reportedly exist in private collections. Others, however, have seemingly been lost. Given their tremendous similarity to regular Type 1 proof nickels, it is not impossible that some may lie unattributed.

No trial strikings have been reported with the Type 2 reverse. The one possible exception is the piece which surfaced along with the five 1913 Liberty Head Nickels in 1920. This was coined in an alloy of 95% copper, 5% nickel and zinc.[75] Its origin is unknown and, like its five brothers, it was probably produced without authorization to serve as a delicacy. This coin is has been owned for decades by eminent numismatist Eric P. Newman, who retained it along with the presentation case that once contained this piece, the five 1913 Liberty Head Nickels and two additional Buffalo Nickels. One was a proof of the regular Type 1. The second was one of the prototype coins lacking Fraser's initial F. The eight coins were arranged in two rows of four within a leather-covered, satin-lined case. Mr. Newman generously permitted the author to examine his bronze 1913 nickel at the 1999 convention of the American Numismatic Association in Chicago. It is quite ordinary in all respects, save for its composition.

1913 Type 2 Nickel struck in the cent alloy
(Eric P. Newman, Photo by American Numismatic Association Museum)

First prototype, coined January 13, 1913, 4.996 grams: Breen 2584
(Smithsonian Institution, National Numismatic Collection, photo by Douglas A. Mudd)

First prototype, second example, 5.489 grams: Breen 2584
(SINNC, Mudd)

Second prototype, coined February 13, 1913, 5.037 grams: Breen 2585
(SINNC, Mudd)

Second prototype, second example, 5.396 grams: Breen 2585
(SINNC, Mudd)

Footnotes to Chapter 1

[1] *The Numismatist.* September-
   October 1909
[2] National Archives, Record Group
   104, File 305927
[3] NA, RG 104, File 305310
[4] ibid
[5] ibid
[6] ibid
[7] *The Numismatist,* January 1912
[8] NA, RG 104, File 305310
[9] ibid
[10] ibid
[11] NA, RG 104, File 308449
[12] ibid
[13] NA, RG 104, File 305310
[14] ibid
[15] ibid
[16] ibid
[17] ibid
[18] ibid
[19] ibid
[20] NA, RG 104, File 308449
[21] NA, RG 104, File 305310
[22] ibid
[23] ibid
[24] ibid
[25] ibid
[26] ibid
[27] ibid
[28] ibid
[29] ibid
[30] ibid

[31] ibid
[32] ibid
[33] ibid
[34] ibid
[35] ibid
[36] ibid
[37] ibid
[38] ibid
[39] NA, RG 104, File 308449
[40] ibid
[41] *The Numismatist,* May 1913
[42] NA, RG 104, File 305310
[43] ibid
[44] ibid
[45] ibid
[46] ibid
[47] ibid
[48] ibid
[49] *The Numismatist,* March 1938
[50] Anderson, Burnett. "Senator
   requests Buffalo nickel reissue
   in silver."
[51] Ganz, David L. "Turnover Time
   At The Mint"
[52] Sidman, Ray. "Lucas
   Spearheads Commemorative
   Coin Bill."
[53] Van Ryzin, Robert. "The Buffalo
   Nickel Hoax"
[54] NA, RG 104, File 305310
[55] *The Numismatist,* February
   1935

[56] Dary, David A. *The Buffalo Book*
[57] Van Ryzin
[58] *The Numismatist,* December
   1915
[59] Breen, Walter. *Walter Breen's
   Complete Encyclopedia of U. S.
   and Colonial Coins*
[60] Ratzman, Leonard J. "The
   Buffalo Nickel, A 50-Year-Old
   Mystery"
[61] author's interview with Mrs.
   Curnen, 1993
[62] Morris, Joseph F. (editor). *James
   Earle Fraser*
[63] Barsness, Larry. *The Bison in Art*
[64] Reed, Fred. "Lincoln Lore:
   Buffalo Nickel Designer Had A
   Penchant For Honest Abe"
[65] Cohen, Annette R. and Ray M.
   Druley, Editors. "Fraser Plaster
   Models Sold at Auction"
[66] Taxay, Don. *The U. S. Mint and
   Coinage*
[67] ibid
[68] NA, RG 104, File 305310
[69] Taxay
[70] NA, RG 104, File 305310
[71] ibid
[72] ibid
[73] Taxay
[74] Breen
[75] Taxay

CHAPTER 2

Collecting
Buffalo Nickels

Though countless Americans saved one or more pieces of the Indian Head/Buffalo Nickel upon its release in 1913, there doesn't appear to have been widespread interest in collecting the entire series by date and mint. There were, of course, those established collectors who purchased one or two examples of every issue, buying them annually from the individual mints at just face value plus postage, but this series did not gain a devoted following until the mid-1930s.

Two events occurred almost simultaneously that together served to create a broad market for these coins. The first was the creation of a low-mintage issue at the San Francisco Mint in 1931. While there had been a number of low-mintage dates before, such as 1915-S and 1926-S, these had been quietly released into circulation without much notice from the hobby, making uncirculated pieces quite scarce in later years. This rarity actually had the short-term effect of discouraging collecting. The 1,200,000 nickels struck at the San Francisco Mint in 1931 were a different story. The Depression-racked economy of that year did not demand any additional coinage of nickels, and these coins went into storage. By this time, hobby publications such as *The Numismatist* had begun to publish monthly and annual coinage figures, and the small mintage of 1931-S nickels, performed mostly at the end of the year, drew some notice. Not having been distributed to commercial banks, these coins remained mostly unavailable, as were the 1931-S cents for the same reason. This artificial scarcity created a speculative market in what appeared to be rare coins.

When they were finally released in 1934-35, both issues were immediately hoarded by speculators who managed to amass very large quantities. Offered as singles or in roll lots, the 1931-S cents and nickels found ready

buyers, while they remained genuinely rare in circulation. The timing of this development couldn't have been better, as the demand for modern issues was growing rapidly.

This brings us to the second key development in the popularity of collecting Buffalo Nickels. The very first coin albums appeared late in 1928 when Martin Luther Beistle introduced this new product. M. L. Beistle was a manufacturer of paper novelty items in Shippensburg, Pennsylvania, and the coin album was a natural blending of his business and his coin collecting hobby. Beistle's concept was one that's become very familiar today. He

(The Numismatist, May 1929)

devised cardboard pages pierced with holes into which coins could be placed. The coins were then secured within their holes by celluloid slides that were inserted into the end of each page. Finally, the pages were pierced with holes in their margins for mounting within a ring binder built to suit.

Though Beistle's product was somewhat crude by current standards, it was the concept that sold it. Previously, collectors had kept their coins in expensive, wooden cabinets with felt-lined drawers or had simply placed them in paper envelopes of an appropriate size. Beistle's album design was promising enough that prominent New York City dealer Wayte Raymond bought the rights to it around 1931 and began marketing these albums under the National Brand.

National albums were still a bit expensive, and their target market was the established coin collector who was already well versed in the hobby. Though many albums were sold to collectors of Buffalo Nickels, the real popularity of this series began when simpler and less expensive coin holders became available. This became a reality in 1934 with the introduction of the first coin board. Consisting of simply a paper-backed sheet of 11" x 14" cardboard pierced with holes of the appropriate size and lettered to suit, the coin board was the invention of J. K. Post in Neenah, Wisconsin. Post contracted with Whitman Publishing Company in nearby Racine to manufacture the boards. A seller of games, jigsaw puzzles and children's books, Whitman was well suited to mass-producing inexpensive paper products for hobbyists. The first boards were made for collecting Indian Head or Lincoln Cents, but titles for Liberty Head and Buffalo Nickels were introduced in 1935 and proved to be an immediate success.

So successful, in fact, were the boards that Post was nearly overwhelmed by the demand. Whitman Publishing, impressed by the amount of product Post was moving, bought the rights from him in 1936. From that point onward, Whitman was at the forefront of

(The Numismatist, February 1931)

the coin collecting supply business, and it remains one of the key players to this day. Though the Buffalo Nickel series terminated in 1938 and fit quite neatly on a single board, the ongoing Lincoln Cent and Mercury Dime series soon outgrew this format. By the early 1940s, the large boards had been replaced by the three-panel folders so familiar to later generations of collectors.

*   *   *   *   *

While the appearance of the coin board in 1934 did indeed revolutionize the coin hobby, making it affordable to most Americans and creating a previously unimagined demand for circulated coins, it was really Beistle's albums that first put the Buffalo Nickel series in the spotlight. Until the late 1920s it was quite rare to find ads offering modern coins by date and mint. While there were a few people quietly collecting these pieces, the premiums attached to them evidently didn't merit the placing of ads in *The Numismatist*. It was in 1928 that the first offerings of current series appeared. These began with Indian Head and Lincoln Cents but were extended to Buffalo Nickels by that fateful year of 1931. The Beistle/Raymond albums provided a means of collecting these coins, and the premiums attached to uncirculated pieces grew steadily during the 1930s.

The primary suppliers of modern coins by date and mint were F. C. C. Boyd in New York City, A. C. Gies in Pittsburgh and William Pukall in Union City, New Jersey. All were in businesses that gave them access to large quantities of coins, and they financed their own collecting in part by placing these modern pieces with mail-order customers. In order to promote sales of his albums, Wayte Raymond ultimately bought out these individual hoarders, and he remained a primary source of both common and scarce issues until his death in 1956. His estate included large quantities of these pieces, and they were wholesaled to various dealers for the next several years. The hoards have long since been dispersed, and roll quantities of any coins before the 1930s have become something of a rarity.

It's ironic that during the Great Depression of the 1930s, a time when the prices of truly rare coins were temporarily in decline, there were startling advances in prices for what were essentially common coins. These included the many commemorative issues of the period, as well as what were then current series such as Buffalo Nickels and Lincoln Cents. This contradiction reflected a demographic shift in the coin collecting hobby, as many newcomers began checking their pocket change for dates needed to fill their boards. This became a popular family hobby, though it was still essentially a male activity. As these new collectors grew in sophistication, they began to seek uncirculated pieces to replace their "hole fillers," and the prices for mint state Buffalo Nickels and other current or recent series rose accordingly.

The 1940s saw a tremendous growth in the coin collecting hobby, due to the unique nature of the wartime economy. Those remaining on the homefront earned unprecedented wages, often working multiple shifts or extensive overtime. At the same time, the production of most consumer goods was either restricted or completely curtailed in favor of items essential to the war effort. Unable to buy many of the things they desired, but with pockets bulging, most Americans spent their money on entertainment, one of the few pleasures that remained in abundant supply. Sales of movie tickets reached a climax during this period, and hobbies of every kind experienced unprecedented growth. The collecting of both stamps and coins soared in popularity, though the rationing of paper supplies occasionally interfered with the production of albums and guide books.

New records were set at nearly every coin auction during the years 1943-48, and it was only toward the end of the decade that the coin market entered a slump. Recovering by 1952, the growth that followed actually dwarfed the expansion of the 1940s, as there were now no restrictions whatsoever on the supply of hobby products. New albums and holders made of plastic rivaled the cardboard types as early as 1945, though paper-based albums predominated through the 1950s. Joining Whitman in the manufacture and sale of coin albums and folders were the Daniel Stamp Company (DANSCO), Harris (of stamp collecting fame), Meghrig, Library of Coins, Shoreline (one of the many Whitman lookalikes), Harold Cohn (HARCO) and dozens of regional and local brands completely forgotten

---

Buffalo Nickel Uncirculated Five Cent Pieces.

1913	$ .15
1913 S and D each	.45
1914	.35
1914 S and D each	.55
1915	.40
1915 S and D each	.55
1916	.35
1916 D	.55
1916 S	.45
1917	.30
1917 D	.45
1917 S	.55
1918	.30
1918 S and D each	.55
1919	**.30**
1919 S and D each	.55
1920	.30
1920 S and D each	.55
1923	.40
1923 S	.55
1924	.30
1924 S and D each	.40
1925	.30
1925 S and D each	.40
1926	.20
1926 S and D each	.40
1927	.20
1927 S	.50
1928	.15
1928 D	.20
1928 S	.30
1929	.15
1929 D	.20

Uncirculated and Proof of Liberty Head Nickels at reasonable prices.

WM. PUKALL,

911 Eighteenth St.,   Union City, N. J.

(The Numismatist, March 1931)

today. The peak production of albums coincided with the apex of popular coin collecting in the years 1958-64, when the coin hobby was frequently the subject of media attention.

Throughout this period the Buffalo Nickel series remained a perennial favorite. As these coins gradually disappeared from circulation during the 1950s, the rush was on to secure even the more common dates. Many of the pieces still to be found were, in fact, already dateless. This prompted the introduction of various chemicals for restoring dates on anonymous nickels, one of which is still made today. This has as its active ingredient a mild acid that etches the surface of the coin's metal. Since the striking process work-hardened the metal to a degree that varied with the depth of the die cavity, the etching process mimics this action, revealing a shallow image of the date. Though coins having restored dates carried little or no premium, such was the mania for collecting Buffalo Nickels in the 1950s and early '60s that thousands of collectors simply couldn't resist hunting for treasure by this means.

* * * * *

The coin hobby entered a period of decline beginning in the mid-1960s, due to a variety of causes. The speculative market that developed in rolls and even bags of recent coins collapsed in the latter months of 1964, leaving many of the fair-weather collectors strapped for cash and quite disillusioned. Beginning in the fall of 1965, coins formerly made of silver were quickly replaced by ones of copper-nickel, and all remaining silver pieces were driven from circulation within two to three years. Sales of proof sets were suspended from 1965 through 1967, and in their place were offered overpriced Special Mint Sets of mediocre quality.

These factors drove away many of the people attracted to coin collect-

ing during the 1950s and early '60s whose primary motivation had been greed, but it also ruined the hobby for countless kids and adults who were actually having fun filling their folders from pocket change. As for Buffalo Nickels, these were already becoming scarce after 1960, but the disappearance of silver coins spurred efforts to remove the last remaining pieces. By 1970 it was quite rare to find even dateless pieces.

Serious collectors who had already committed themselves to buying quality coins at premium prices were largely unaffected by the exodus of casual hobbyists, and they may have even viewed the lower prices as a welcome opportunity. Even so, this bursting of the coin bubble was a blow from which the greater hobby has never fully recovered. Only the recent popularity of the 50-states quarter dollar program offers hope of a widespread coin collecting revival. This is evident in the great variety and visibility of albums for these coins. Not since the 1960s have so many coin folders and display boards appeared for sale in general retail stores, a welcome development indeed.

* * * * *

One of the interesting by-products of

(The Numismatist, 1933)

the coin collecting mania of the late 1950s and early '60s was the great fluctuation in prices for certain issues within the Buffalo Nickel series. In the first edition of this book, published in 1992, I noted that many of the semi-key dates such as 1920-S and 1927-S had peaked in value in the lower grades during the early 1960s. The values of these coins in grades Good through Fine either declined or remained stagnant after that time and had still not recovered thirty years later. I offered little hope for upward price movement, as it seemed these coins were not wanted by anyone at that time.

When the popularity of collecting coins was widespread, these pieces commanded relatively large premiums. The subsequent decline in values suffered by these issues can be traced to a major change in the nature of the coin collecting hobby. The inclination of collectors during the 1950s and early 1960s was to hunt for needed dates by examining pocket change and by searching rolls obtained from a nearby bank. With most collectors living in the East or the Midwest, S-Mint nickels seemed particularly elusive and acquired a peculiar mystique. All that was necessary to dispel this illusion was to speak with dealers in the West, most of whom possessed these dates in abundance. Such coins had been widely hoarded in low grades during the 1940s and '50s and were therefore

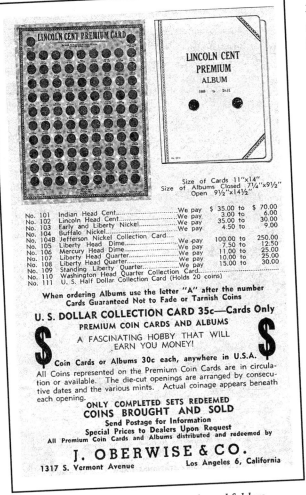

Advertisement for coin boards and folders (The Numismatist, 1944)

more common than was generally believed.

As the 1960s passed, a new generation of collectors who had never known the thrill of assembling a Buffalo Nickel collection from circulation entered the market. While previous generations had been content to purchase the semi-key dates in low grades, as these coins matched the ones already acquired from circulation, the new collectors quickly learned to seek only higher grade pieces. There was a particular emphasis on mint state coins, as the stellar gains they'd made since the 1940s became part of the new investment climate. At the same time that the "pocket change" generation was being driven away from coin collecting, the "deep pocket" generation was pushing up the prices of coins grading XF and higher. The knowledge that low-grade, semi-key coins were overrated, combined with a dwindling market for such grades, had the inevitable effect of depressing the prices for several dates.

When I wrote the first edition of this book in 1992, it seemed that this trend was irreversible. In fact, most Buffalo Nickels in the grades of Good through Fine have made impressive gains during the intervening years. While forty years of inflation has proved these coins to have been a bad investment overall, there are signs that the collecting of even well worn Buffalo Nickels is on the rise.

*   *   *   *   *

The collecting of Buffalo Nickels entered a new period of sophistication during the 1970s, along with the coin market in general. New entrants into the coin hobby were often lured by the prospect of profiting from an investment in rare coins, and most dealers shifted their sales pitches in this direction. Prices rose rapidly during the latter part of the decade, as coins were increasingly viewed as a hedge against double-digit inflation. The coin market eventually overheated, and this led to a sharp decline in the value of mint state and proof coins during the early 1980s. While some collectors and investors dropped out, often hastily selling their coins at a loss, there remained a greater number of people active in the coin hobby/business than there had been a decade earlier.

One of the less desirable developments to come from a general increase in values since the

1940s was the appearance of numerous counterfeit and altered coins. Before the 1970s, most such pieces were crude and did not pose a threat to knowledgeable buyers. The science of counterfeit detection was in its infancy, however, and it was not long before more sophisticated fakes were devised. This led to the creation of the American Numismatic Association Certification Service in the 1970s. Its initial role was merely to authenticate coins and attribute varieties, but the ever-increasing values led to disputes over grading. Grading guides existed for circulated coins, but most of the abuses and complaints centered around mint state and proof pieces, for which their were no published standards.

By 1979 ANACS had begun issuing grading certificates for coins, and these included photographs of the piece in question. The intent of this service was simply to arbitrate disputes over specific pieces on an as-needed basis, but coin dealers quickly realized that these grading certificates could be used as marketing tools. Soon, it became almost essential to have valuable coins certified by ANACS, and this service was the primary source of the ANA's revenue

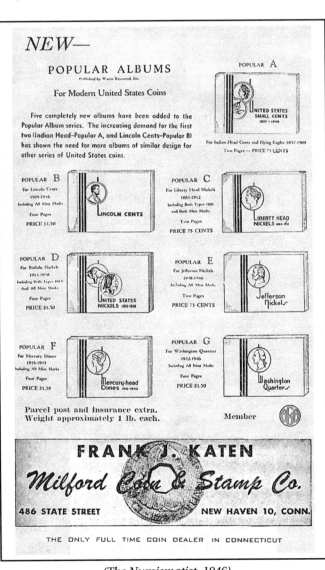

(The Numismatist, 1946)

throughout much of the 1980s.

The success of ANACS led to the next logical development in the marketing of coins. Though each certificate was accompanied by photos of the subject coin, there always existed the risk that the coin depicted was not the one being offered for sale. Two untoned and uncirculated coins of the same date and mint could appear quite similar in a photograph, and substitutions were sometimes made at the expense of the buyer. This weakness was addressed with the creation in 1986 of the Professional Coin Grading Service, a commercial venture that placed both the certificate and the coin inside a sealed holder. Neither could be swapped without it being evident from examination of the holder. PCGS was followed just a year later by Numismatic Guaranty Corporation (NGC), and several other commercial grading services now compete with these two major players. ANACS was sold by the ANA to a commercial operator in 1990, and in its place was established the American Numismatic Association Authentication Bureau (ANAAB). While ANAAB still provides authentication, attribution and conservation services, it no longer grades coins.

*   *   *   *   *

The impact of these developments on the collecting of Buffalo Nickels has been profound. While there are still many who place circulated pieces inside traditional paper-based albums or plastic display frames, most serious collectors now prefer their coins to be certified and encapsulated. These encapsulations are stored upright within plastic boxes made specifically to fit them. Publication of the grading services' certified populations by date, mint and grade has lessened the perceived rarity of some issues, such as 1931-S, while revealing other dates to be important condition rarities.

The latest development in certified grading is the collection registry, in which collectors can have their sets compared and ranked against those submitted by other individuals. This activity is greatly facilitated by the widespread growth and acceptance of the Internet and the prevalence of home computers having Internet access. Easy scanning of coin images and posting of these images at registry websites add to the collecting experience.

The prevalence of certified coins, with their guaranteed authenticity, has all but driven out counterfeit and altered pieces. These are still a menace at small coin shows, country auctions and the like, but both dealers and collectors are careful to have valuable coins certified. Counterfeit and altered coins still turn up with some regularity when collections assembled between about 1950 and 1980 are brought to market, so caution is urged when purchasing uncertified, key-date coins.

While much of the fun of assembling collections within albums has been lost to the present generation of collectors, the coins themselves enjoy far greater protection from the environment. Even the best made albums leave coins somewhat vulnerable to mechanical damage from the albums' moving slides and subject them to chemical reactions with both the cardboard and the atmosphere. This point was driven home not long ago when the famed collection of the late John Jay Pittman was offered at auction. Stored for decades in one of the Raymond albums, his Buffalo Nickel set included numerous coins that would have been gems had not their edges developed signs of corrosion. In some instances this corrosion extended to the coins' rims and facing surfaces, too. While the coins were accurately described and sold for prices that reflected their problems, for one who treasures Buffalo Nickels it was a heartbreaking experience to see them impaired that way.

*   *   *   *   *

As this is written in 2000, the collecting of Buffalo Nickels has never been more popular. I've received calls almost weekly from collectors and dealers hoping to secure a copy of this book's first edition, which has been sold out for several years. Since 1995, I've been teaching a class on this series at the ANA's annual Summer Conference in Colorado Springs, usually in partnership with Buffalo collector extraordinaire, Bill Fivaz. The level of enthusiasm expressed by our students is very gratifying and bodes well for the future. This is by far the best educated generation of coin collectors in terms of both historical and technical knowledge.

Perhaps the most rapid area of growth for the Buffalo Nickel series is in the field of variety collecting. Also being released this year is a new edition of *The Cherrypicker's Guide to Rare Die Varieties*, by Bill Fivaz and J. T. Stanton. This popular title has been sold out for some years, and the fourth edition includes many new listing within the Buffalo Nickel section. Prominent among these for the first time are several two-feathers varieties, an area largely overlooked by variety specialists until recently. A perusal of the Bibliography offered in Appendix C will reveal other titles of a specialized or general nature pertaining to Buffalo Nickels.

While the number of albums being produced for this series has declined since the 1960s, each of the current manufacturers includes Buffalo Nickels within its line of titles. Albums or folders for collecting this series have thus been in print continually since 1935. Old collections still come back onto the market with some frequency. Of course, most of these are incomplete sets of well-worn pieces acquired 40-50 years ago from circulation or purchased inexpensively from mail-order dealers or local coin shops. The offering of a high-grade collection, complete with the rare issues, is an important event and seldom occurs outside of major auction houses.

*   *   *   *   *

As a footnote to this look at collecting Buffalo Nickels, I'd like to relate my own experi-ences with this series. I began collecting from circulation around 1965, starting with partial sets of Lincoln Cents and Buffalo Nickels I acquired from my older brother. Like most kids of that generation, he'd played at collecting coins for a short time before moving on to other childhood amusements. I still have this incomplete set, which at some point was trans-ferred from its original blue folder to a Whitman Bookshelf album.

When I first took over this collection it included seven coins, mostly Philadelphia Mint pieces from the 1920s and '30s. Over the years I've come close to completing this set through a variety of means, most of them unplanned. I managed to add just three coins from actual circulation, these being 1918-S, 1920-S and 1937-D. The first two were so worn that it took some time to make out their dates, and they'd probably been rejected by a number of less per-sistent collectors before me. The last piece bore a sharp date and, sadly, four complete legs.

When I finally realized that the remain-ing coins would not be found in circulation, I began buying the needed issues from dealers' junk boxes in whatever condition I found them. This filled about two-thirds of the album before I grew weary of ugly, problem coins and just put the set away. In the meantime, I matured as a collector and developed a taste for nicer coins. My interests shifted toward early United States series such as Bust and Seated Liberty coins, and numismatics for me became more than just filling holes in an album.

It wasn't until the mid-1980s that I came back to collecting Buffalo Nickels. On a lark, I had put together a one-a-year set of nicely matched XF-AU coins in problem-free, original condition. This was then expanded with the addition of various D- and S-Mint coins needed for a full set. I learned early on that premium prices were necessary to secure attractive examples of the key and semi-key dates, and within a few years I had a very pleas-ing set. Only the coins from 1934 onward were uncirculated, though most of the remaining pieces were deceptively close to mint state. Many of these were featured as plate coins in the first edition of this book, and readers will observe that some of the photos in Chapter 6 have been upgraded from the ones I provided last time.

After the book came out in 1992, there seemed little to be gained from holding onto a set of coins that was already complete and that I couldn't afford to upgrade. I decided to sell my collection of Buffaloes privately by offering it to those who would most appreciate the coins, the purchasers of my book. Unfortunately, I hadn't begun saving names and addresses until several dozen books had already been shipped, so the mailing list I had was incomplete. This proved to be no problem, however, since the collection was completely sold in one evening. I was surprised at how quickly I received telephone calls wanting to buy one or more of the coins from my list. The sixth caller wanted to buy the entire collection intact, but it was already too late. He settled for buying all the remaining pieces, and many other persons were disappointed over the next few days.

This isn't quite the end of the story, since there was still my childhood set of Buffalo Nickels. While I've made no direct effort to complete the collection for nearly thirty years, a number of missing coins have come to me by way of another hobby of mine -- collecting coin albums. I pursue this activity with the vigor that most numismatists reserve exclusively for actual coins. In the course of acquiring desired albums, it's sometimes necessary to buy them with the coins still in place. This is no hardship when it comes to incomplete sets of Lincolns and Buffaloes, since the keys are invariably missing, and the remaining coins are quite inexpensive. By buying these sets, however, I've managed to fill in some holes in both series, the only United States coins I still collect by date and mint. I've found that many dealers are quite indiscriminate about values when they have a chance to unload partial sets. In fact, that's how I got my 1931-S nickel in VG for just thirty cents. Neither the dealer nor I noticed that it was in the wrong hole!

CHAPTER 3

Gallery of Errors

Some error coins of the Indian Head/Buffalo Nickel type are not especially rare. Off-centered or broadstruck coins, for example, are available in circulated grades at a moderate cost. The errors shown here, however, include some of the most spectacular examples known.

Among the coins pictured are high grade examples of dates that are scarce as normal strikes. In the context of error coinage, they are extraordinarily rare. These coins were provided by several enthusiastic collectors of Buffalo Nickel errors. They include Bob Entlich, Ken Hill and Norm Talbert, and I'm quite indebted to them for their generosity

1913-P Type 1: The planchet as made was laminated. An imperfect mixing of the alloy led to peeling at the surface, and this caused the coin to be broadstruck outside of the restraining collar. *(Mid-American Rare Coin Auctions)*

1913 (type & mint unknown): The cupronickel alloy used for coining five cent pieces was very difficult to mix and did not always bond properly. Here, a coin has split after striking. A similar piece showing only the reverse once existed, but it has become separated and may be lost or in the hands of another owner. *(Norm Talbert)*

1913 Type 2 (mint unknown): The planchet was punched out of the trailing edge or side of the metal strip, leaving a straightedge clip. This led to the nickel being broadstruck. *(Mid-American Rare Coin Auctions)*

1913 Type 2 (mint unknown): This coin was struck on a planchet cut from the tapered, leading edge of the metal strip. This tapering facilitates the feeding of the strip into the draw bench which then reduces it to the proper thickness. *(Bob Entlich)*

1913-D Type 2: This nickel was struck 20% off-centered and circulated for some years. (*author*)

1916-D: Broadstruck. The protruding flange or "railroad rim" visible in the obverse photo reveals that Buffalo Nickels were coined with the reverse die in the upper or hammer position. This flange always extends along the top surface of the restraining collar. (*Talbert*)

1914-P: Here is another example of a planchet splitting after striking. It's rare to find both halves of the coin. (*Ken Hill*)

1916-S: A lamination which was present on the obverse of this nickel when struck has peeled away, leaving an indistinct image underneath. (*Talbert*)

1917-P: This nickel was coined about 15% off-centered. (*Hill*)

1917-P: A centered, broadstruck coin, this piece was produced outside the collar and is unusually large for this type of error. *(Hill)*

1917-S: Struck twice, this extremely rare error is also notable for the scarcity of this date in mint state. *(Hill)*

1918-D: A silver dime planchet was inadvertently fed into a press which was striking nickels, and this piece was the result. *(Entlich)*

1918-D: Punched out of a portion of the strip which had already been punched twice, the planchet was double clipped before striking. Note the indistinct areas opposite the clips. Normal coins which have been cut in an attempt to fake this error will not display such diagnostic weakness. *(Mid-American Rare Coin Auctions)*

1918-D: Another scarce date in mint state, this nickel is about 25% off-centered. Note how error coins are often more sharply struck than regular pieces of the same date/mint. *(Hill)*

1919-P: Struck once, this coin briefly adhered to the upper die, then fell onto the lower die after flipping over, finally receiving a second strike outside the collar. This is known as a "flip-over double strike". *(Mid-American Rare Coin Auctions)*

1919-S: Struck off-centered, this nickel is nevertheless more sharply detailed than most examples of this date! *(Mid-American Rare Coin Auctions)*

1919 (mint unknown): It appears that two planchets were struck one atop the other, each receiving an impression from just one die. The obverse impression then split. Note "chin whiskers" die clash. *(Hill)*

1920 (mint unknown): Here is a planchet which split prior to striking. Since the planchet was so thin, the dies barely made contact with it, leaving ghostly images of the Indian and the bison. *(Talbert)*

1920-P: Broadstruck through a piece of cloth or some other foreign material, this nickel possesses a partial collar or "railroad rim". *(Mid-American Rare Coin Auctions)*

1920-P: Struck on a cent planchet.
(Entlich)

1920-P: Struck off-centered.
(Talbert)

1920-P: This nickel was struck twice. The second impression occurred after another planchet had been fed, nearly obliterating the reverse design. It features a partial collar which is slightly visible in the obverse photo. *(Mid-American Rare Coin Auctions)*

1920-D: The planchet was punched from the ragged end of a strip, leaving it incomplete. The lack of sufficient metal compression in the area opposite this gap resulted in the weakness evident in both photos. *(Entlich)*

1920-S: Not completely ejected from the dies after the first strike, this nickel was struck again off-centered. *(Entlich)*

1921-P: This nickel was struck on a cent planchet. *(Hill)*

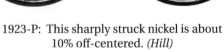

1923-P: This sharply struck nickel is about 10% off-centered. *(Hill)*

1924-P: Off-centered. *(Talbert)*

1924 (mint unknown): Buffalo Nickels struck this far off-centered are rare. *(Hill)*

1929-D: The planchet for this nickel was punched from the ragged, trailing edge of the metal strip. In addition, the obverse displays some deep laminations. *(Entlich)*

1934-P: Off-centered. *(Talbert)*

1934-P: Another off-centered coin, this one quite lustrous. *(Hill)*

1935-P: The planchet for this coin was punched from the end of the strip. *(Hill)*

1935-P: A double-clipped planchet led to this broadstrike. Ironically, the sharpness of detail is superior to that seen on most nickels of this date. *(Mid-American Rare Coin Auctions)*

1935 (mint unknown): The same sequence of events occurred with this coin as with the one preceding. The example shown here, however, displays more typical detail. *(Entlich)*

1935-P: A cud appears at 6 o'clock obverse where a portion of the die has broken away allowing metal to flow into the gap. In addition, this coin has been struck through some foreign material adhering to the die, probably as a result of the cud. *(Talbert)*

1935 (mint unknown): Known as a brockage, this error occurred when a previously struck coin adhered to the reverse (upper) die. The obverse of the adhering coin then functioned as a second obverse die, conveying a transposed image of itself to the coin shown. *(Entlich)*

1935-P: Off-centered strike. *(Talbert)*

1935-P: This nickel failed to eject from the dies after being struck. Instead, it rotated a few degrees and was struck a second time. *(Talbert)*

1936 (mint unknown): Two blank planchets were fed into the press simultaneously, one centered atop the obverse (lower) die and the other off-centered and lying atop the first. When both were struck, the second planchet masked a portion of the first, which is shown here. *(Entlich)*

1936-P: Broadstruck. *(Talbert)*

1936-P: Flipover double strikes are exceedingly rare, and this is one of the nicest. *(Hill)*

1937-P: Struck off-centered. *(Talbert)*

Philadelphia Mint (date unknown): This error is called a capped-die, or simply a cap. A struck coin adhered to the reverse (upper) die, while the coin's obverse was repeatedly pounded against incoming planchets. With each successive blow, the coin spread outward, eventually wrapping itself around the reverse die before falling off or being manually removed by the press operator. *(Entlich)*

Philadelphia Mint (date unknown): This nickel was struck on a Peruvian five-centavos planchet, which dates it to 1918, 1919, 1923 or 1926. *(Hill)*

Philadelphia Mint (date unknown): This coin was struck off-centered on an incomplete planchet. *(Hill)*

Philadelphia Mint (date unknown): More than 50% off-centered, this nickel is a high-grade error. *(Hill)*

Date and mint unknown: Two planchets were overlapping when struck, this one receiving an off-centered impression. *(Hill)*

CHAPTER 4

Counterfeit & Altered Coins

Counterfeit & Altered Coins

As long as there have been coins there have been counterfeiters, and the Buffalo Nickel was not immune to this threat. As early as April of 1913, *The Numismatist* could report that "Already the counterfeiters are at work on the new five cent piece, and a number of leaden imitations have been placed in circulation." Cast lead counterfeits of the Buffalo Nickel may still be found in accumulations of old coins, and a couple of these are illustrated here more for amusement purposes than to educate. Such relics of a bygone era are far too crude to fool most collectors. More dangerous is the counterfeit or altered coin intended for the numismatic marketplace. These are generally more sophisticated in technique than circulating fakes.

Quality counterfeits that could deceive experienced authenticators are thus far unknown for the Buffalo Nickel series. Or, perhaps, they have not yet been detected. A more urgent concern is the problem of clever alterations of otherwise genuine coins. The simplest method of adding value to a common date in the series is to apply a mintmark to a Philadelphia Mint coin.

For instance, 1924-P is only slightly scarce as a date, yet when an S mintmark is added it becomes one of the keys to the series in grades VF and higher. This can be done by removing the mintmark from a common date San Francisco Mint nickel such as 1936-S and bonding it in the appropriate position on the P-Mint coin. The mintmark can be soldered on or cemented with epoxy. This usually results in a mintmark that has the appearance of floating on the coin's surface rather than flowing directly into it as a genuine mintmark would. Of course, the skill with which this operation is performed will determine its relative success. Some very deceptive examples have been found. Included in this rogue's gallery are 1913-S Type 2, 1915-S, 1918/7-D (altered date, as well), 1920-D, 1920-S, 1921-S, 1924-S, 1925-D, 1925-S, 1926-D, 1926-S and 1927-S.

Another method through which a mintmark may be added is more elaborate. An entire section of a coin bearing the desired mintmark is cut from it and a similar portion is removed from another piece that possesses the desired date. A swap is then made, leaving one coin that bears a valuable combination of date and mint. Since the amount of rotation between obverse and reverse dies will vary from one nickel to another, the section removed is cut only halfway through the thickness of each coin, thus leaving the corresponding portion of the obverse intact. Of course, this method will leave obvious signs of tooling where the cut was made and along the coin's edge. Attempts to smooth out this alteration will always be imperfect, and further tricks to conceal the deception such as the application of polishing, artificial toning or tiny nicks and scratches may also be employed.

Similar in concept but distinctive in method is the halving of two entire nickels to make up one valuable piece. Such an example is the 1926-S Buffalo Nickel shown here. It is really comprised of a 1926-P obverse bonded to the reverse of a common and extremely well struck S-Mint coin from the 1930s. The seam along its edge is all too obvious, once one has thought to check this third surface. Unfortunately, most collectors and dealers do not check the edge when a coin is sealed in a tight-fitting holder. This particular specimen was one of several dated 1913-S Type 2, 1914-D and 1926-S that were deceptively sold to some very knowledgeable dealers before they began to suspect that these key dates were suddenly becoming too common.

Yet another variation on this theme is to hollow out most of one entire coin, leaving something that resembles a shallow bottle cap. Another nickel having the desired date or mintmark (depending on whether obverse or reverse is needed) is then turned down on a lathe, reducing its diameter enough that it may be inserted into the bottle cap. The seam is less likely to be detected with this method, as it's hidden in the coin's rim and can be more easily smoothed over.

By far the most diabolically clever alterations to appear for the Buffalo Nickel series are the infamous "embossed" mintmarks that turned up in the early 1980s. Several key date issues were simulated by pushing up mintmarks from within the coins. A common date such as 1919-P was made into a scarce 1919-D by having a small hole drilled into its edge directly adjacent to where the mintmark should appear. A pair of narrow pliers was then used to raise the mintmark. One jaw bearing a mintmark in relief was inserted into the hole, while the other jaw was wrapped in some protective material such as hard leather or plastic and placed against the mintmark area of the nickel (ANAAB). When the handles of the pliers were squeezed, the inside jaw pushed an impression of the mintmark up through the thin layer of metal between the hole and the coin's surface.

The result was an extremely deceptive mintmark that blended directly into the coin's field as would a genuine mintmark. The only obvious sign that an alteration had occurred was a series of tooling marks on the nickel's edge. These could be reduced through smoothing but not entirely eliminated. Dates for which edge examination is mandatory include 1913-S Type 2, 1914-D, 1915-S, 1919-D, 1920-D, 1924-S, 1925-D, 1926-D and 1926-S. Other key dates may yet turn up. Examples of this kind of alteration are illustrated.

In addition to tooling marks, another diagnostic of the embossed alterations is that the mintmark will show the same surface irregularities inherent in the host coin. Note that the metal flow lines present in the die appear also on the highest points of the mintmark for several examples. This is not normal, as the sunken relief of the mintmark in a die should normally protect its highest points from this form of erosion. At the very least, the flow lines will not be as strong as in the coin's field, yet these alterations show very heavy flow lines in their mintmarks. In a more normal situation, the base of the mintmark will be drawn or distorted, as this part receives the greatest effect from metal flow.

Another trick for enhancing the value of a Buffalo Nickel is to raise its grade. This has been done by re-engraving the bison's horn, this being a key element in the grading of Buffalo Nickels. Getting the perfect shape is, of course, quite tricky. Even when the work is done skillfully, an experienced buyer should recognize that the horn detail is inconsistent with the overall wear on the coin. Potentially more deceptive is the engraving of a horn on a less worn coin that was weakly struck and lacking this feature as made.

Collectors and dealers should beware also of faked variety coins. Popular varieties such as the 1918/7-D overdate have been targeted by those who make deceptive alterations. The simplest method to simulate this rare coin is by chasing or manipulating the date of a normal 1918-D nickel so that it has the appearance of an overdate. Such shortcuts produce a very crude product that may deceive the inexperienced but will be no match for those familiar with how the real overdate occurred (see Chapter 6). A more complex method of faking this variety is to make a negative impression of a genuine 1918 nickel obverse and then compress it onto the obverse of a genuine 1917-D nickel. This procedure is difficult to perform successfully, and the end product is again no match for the knowledgeable.

In one instance, a Buffalo Nickel may be made more valuable through the removal of a feature rather than its addition. This coin is, of course, the popular 1937-D "three-legged" nickel. When coin collecting was at its most popular during the late 1950s and early 1960s, this variety was frequently faked by simply grinding off the bison's foreleg. Such alterations deceived many of the less experienced collectors so prevalent then, and they may still pose a problem for newcomers even today. An example of this crude work is shown. In an attempt to cover his work, the coin surgeon has added myriad tiny nicks and has given the coin a deep, artificial toning. Of course, a review of the correct diagnostics for this variety as presented in Chapter 6 will protect potential buyers from these boiler room jobs.

Appealing to a more sophisticated taste is the alleged die trial piece shown. It appears to be a copper impression of a reverse die for the Buffalo Nickel made on some foreign coin. While it is indeed copper, and there is in fact some faint image remaining of a host coin on the plain side, the likelihood of this piece having been struck at a U. S. mint is slim. Not evident from the enlarged photographs is that the die impression is itself slightly oversize, and no explanation exists for how this could be. While the exact nature of this piece remains unknown, it is probably a fabrication made for purposes of whimsy or deception.

Periodic references have been made over the years to the reeded edge cents and nickels of 1937. It is now known that these were alterations of genuine United States coins and were made to be given away or sold as harmless novelties. A more complete explanation may be found in Chapter 6 under the listing for 1937-P.

Another quite innocent, albeit profitable alteration of the Indian Head/Buffalo Nickel was the manufacture of so-called "hobo nickels." Originally, such pieces were carved by hoboes or prisoners from genuine nickels, and they were made both to pass the idle hours and to sell for a small profit. This activity occurred mainly from the 1910s through the 1950s, when coins of this type were still commonplace in circulation. Many such alterations are crude and hardly worthy of notice, while others are truly examples of American folk art at its most amusing. Hobo nickels made after this time are typically mass-produced items of little artistic merit that were not crafted by real hoboes. These are designed to cash in on the popularity of legitimate pieces.

Of the few hobos who can actually be identified with their work, perhaps the most famous and talented was "Bo." His real name was George Washington Hughes, and he lived circa 1900-80. He frequently signed his work with the initials GWH, or simply GH, as on the example shown. His many finely crafted nickels are avidly sought by collectors in this specialized field. Among the few contemporary references to hobo nickels may be found in the June 1918 issue of *The Numismatist*:

> Collectors frequently have brought to their attention coins on which the device has been altered by someone skilled in the use of engravers' tools, giving the piece a humorous or satirical effect. The present type of nickel seems to offer a splendid field for these artists to display their ability, and some ludicrous specimens have been turned out. The latest of these alterations, according to the New York *Times*, is one on which the head of the Indian has been transformed into the head of the Kaiser by the addition of a spiked helmet, and upturned mustache and a close-fitting uniform, with other slight alterations. Some of the altered coins have been found in circulation in Hoboken, N. J., and the Department of Justice has been asked to apprehend the distributors.

Sooner or later, one is likely to encounter an "acid date" nickel. Back when collectors were less conscious of a coin's grade, the name of the game was simply filling the holes in an album or folder. At the time, Buffalo Nickels still circulated, and dateless pieces were frustratingly common. Some enterprising individual discovered that certain acids could etch a coin's surface just enough to bring back a faint image of the date. Bottled under various trade names, this magic formula seemingly gave new life to otherwise useless nickels.

Nickel date restorer was a fixture in coin shops from about the 1950s until quite recently. The reason for its decline is twofold. First, there are fewer coin collectors these days, and their tastes more often lean toward quality rather than quantity. A second factor, one that has appeared only recently, is that dateless Buffalo Nickels now have value to the Native American and western jewelry industry. They are generally worth more dateless than if scarred by acid, and the lure of date restoration is quickly fading.

Finally, there are the completely implausible alterations or fantasy pieces. A good example is the "Texas" nickel illustrated. The coin on the right has been hammered between two strips of leather until its diameter was greatly expanded. The amount of distortion in the design was kept to a minimum, which could fool less experienced collectors. The same may be said of the often seen magician's coins that have two heads or two tails. The editors of question-and-answer columns continue to receive inquiries about these fantasy coins despite efforts to educate collectors that such pieces are fabricated outside of the Mint.

In addition to coins that have been mechanically altered in some manner, there are countless Buffalo Nickels that have been abused in one way or another and have been ruined for numismatic purposes. Among the latter are a dozen coins for whose destruction the author must take full responsibility. When the first edition of this book was issued, I pre-

pared six leather-bound copies that featured actual Buffalo Nickels mounted on their front covers. One each was placed heads or tails, with two coins per book.

Many Buffalo Nickels have simply been cleaned at one time. The manner in which this was done and the severity of the cleaning will determine whether the coin can eventually return to a natural appearance. The major grading services will not certify coins that have obviously been cleaned, while the lesser services will grade them but with qualifying statements that reduce their value.

One notable instance of the widespread cleaning of Buffalo Nickels may be found in the July 1956 issue of *The Numismatist*. Reporting a story from the April 5 edition of the *New York World Telegram*, the following notice appeared:

> As part of the promotion of its new picture "The Last Hunt," MGM planned to affix a shiny buffalo five cent piece to each of 2,000 letters to be sent to foreign distributors. Coin Auditing System, Inc., of New York City undertook the job of providing the coins and reportedly checked a million coins to find 2,000 suitable specimens, which "were put through a burnishing process at a Newark plant to make them nice and shiny. That part of the job cost $17.00."

Cast lead counterfeit with a tin or mercury wash, 1928
(Phelps Dean Witter)

"1926-S" nickel fashioned by halving and then bonding a 1926-P obverse with a common date S-Mint reverse *(Witter)*

Close-up of the counterfeit "two-legged" buffalo *(J.T. Stanton)*

Cast lead counterfeit, 1936 *(Stanton)*

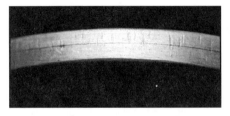

The edge of this muled 1926-S nickel clearly reveals how it was altered *(Witter)*

A close-up of the altered "3-leg" reveals tiny nicks applied to distract a viewer from the alteration *(Fivaz)*

Genuine 1937-D nickel with bison's foreleg removed to achieve the "three-legged" variety *(Bill Fivaz)*

Ira Reed's whimsical novelty, the 1937-P reeded edge nickel *(Talbert)*

The coin was fashioned by George Washington "Bo" Hughes into his interpretation of the Jefferson Nickel. It's signed and dated 1950. *(Fivaz)*

Bo created this likeness of fellow hobo Bert that same year. *(Fivaz)*

Reworking the bison into another image was challenging and less often undertaken by hobos *(Fivaz)*

Coins dipped in acid will be etched and
slightly undersize *(Fivaz)*

Tooling marks on the edge of a "1913-S"
Type 2 with embossed S
*(American Numismatic Association
Authentication Bureau,Fivaz)*

The coin on the right was hammered into its present diameter *(Fivaz)*

Copper whatsit? *(David F. Cieniewicz)*

1913-P Type 2 nickel altered to
1913-S with an embossed mintmark
(ANAAB, courtesy Bill Fivaz)

A second example of tooling marks to create "1913-S" Type 2 with embossed mintmark *(ANAAB,Fivaz)*

1919-D with embossed mintmark
(ANAAB,Fivaz)

1914-D with embossed D
(ANAAB,Fivaz)

1915-S with embossed mintmark *(ANAAB,Fivaz)*

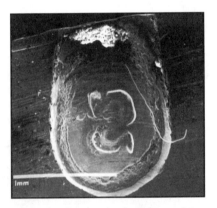

Inside of 1915-S with embossed S
showing cavity for pliers
(ANAAB,Fivaz)

1925-D with embossed D
(ANAAB,Fivaz)

1926-D with embossed D
(ANAAB,Fivaz)

This formerly dateless nickel has
been "restored" with acid
(Author)

1918/7-D with altered date and added D
(ANAAB)

1921-S with added S
(ANAAB)

1924-S with added S
(ANAAB)

1925-D with added D
(ANAAB)

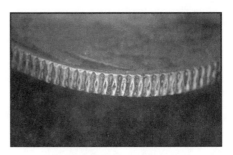

1926-S with added S
(ANAAB)

False (added) reeding on
1913-P Type 1 *(Fivaz)*

CHAPTER 5

Grading Buffalo Nickels

❧

Estimating Rarity

The Buffalo Nickel series is one of the more challenging ones to grade, due to a great variation in the quality of strike. High-grade coins of the Denver and San Francisco Mints may often seem to be well worn, yet the presence of mint luster dispels this illusion. This phenomenon is particularly evident on branch mint coins dated 1917-26. Actual wear first appears on the bison's hipbone and the flank beneath it.

Experience will enable the collector to distinguish between the symptoms of weak striking and legitimate wear. The matter of how to grade and price weakly struck coins remains an ongoing concern. In practice, coins that meet most of the criteria for the assignment of a particular grade will usually receive that grade and may be valued in accordance with current price guides. This is particularly true of dates that are highly in demand but are often found inadequately struck. Well-struck specimens of the same dates will usually command a premium.

An example of how this works may be made of the 1926-S nickel, a date that is very much in demand but which often disappoints potential buyers. In the highly sought grade of Very Fine, this coin should display the full length of the bison's horn, yet it rarely does. More often than not, the pointed end of the horn just fades away indistinctly, blending with the rest of the animal's head as it does on many mint state specimens. In all other respects, the coin still grades VF, and will often be priced as such by the seller. Yet, the great disparity in price between grades F and VF for this date reflects the rarity of such coins with a full horn. In this instance, the buyer must make a judgment call. Take advantage of this opportunity to acquire what is already a scarce coin, or, hold out for that elusive 1926-S nickel with a full horn.

The emphasis placed on the visibility of the bison's horn is not without reason. As may be gleaned from the grading criteria that follow, this feature is the single most important element in establishing the value of a circulated Buffalo Nickel. While the grading standards are written for nickels that display a full strike, they may be applied to all specimens, *provided that some allowance is made for those not fully struck.* The amount of horn visible in grades Very Good through Very Fine is quite important in determining a coin's value, even though it may less useful in establishing a technical grade.

Rather than paraphrase the grading criteria set forth by the American Numismatic Association in its book *Official A.N.A. Grading Standards for United States Coins,* by Kenneth Bressett and the late Abe Kosoff, I have elected to reproduce them verbatim. I must, however, include a cautionary note. It has been my experience that knowledgeable collectors and dealers define a Fine-12 reverse as one that displays two-thirds of the bison's horn, rather than the three-fourths specified by the ANA. This observation is repeated below as a bracketed note. Also, the major grading services (PCGS and NGC) utilize the designation XF instead of EF for the Extremely Fine grade. The meaning of these abbreviations is the same.

ABOUT GOOD (AG-3)

OBVERSE: Design is outlined with nearly all details worn away. Date and motto partially readable but very weak and merging into rim.

REVERSE: Entire design partially worn away. Rim is merged with the letters.

GOOD (G-4)

OBVERSE: Entire design well worn with very little detail remaining in central part. LIBERTY is weak and merged with rim.

REVERSE: Buffalo is nearly flat but is well outlined. Horn does not show. Legend is weak but readable. Rim worn to tops of letters.

VERY GOOD (VG-8)

OBVERSE: Outline of hair is visible at temple and near cheekbone. LIBERTY merges with rim. Date is clear.

REVERSE: Some detail shows in head. Lettering is all clear. Horn is worn nearly flat but is partially visible.

FINE (F-12)

OBVERSE: Three-quarters of details show in hair and braid. LIBERTY is plain.

REVERSE: Major details visible along the back. Horn and tail are smooth but three-quarters visible. [Two-thirds horn visible is the market standard]

VERY FINE (VF-20)

OBVERSE: Hair and cheek show considerable flatness, but all details are clear. Feathers still show partial detail.

REVERSE: Hair on head is worn. Tail and point of horn are visible.

CHOICE VERY FINE (VF-30)

OBVERSE: Hair shows nearly full details. Feathers and braid are worn but sharp.

REVERSE: Head, front leg and hip are worn. Tail shows plainly. Horn is worn but full.

EXTREMELY FINE (EF-40)

OBVERSE: Hair and face are lightly worn but well defined and bold. Slight wear shows on lines of hair braid.

REVERSE: Horn and end of tail are worn but all details are visible.

CHOICE EXTREMELY FINE (EF-45)

OBVERSE: Slight wear shows on the hair above the braid. There is a trace of wear on the temple and hair near cheekbone.

REVERSE: High points of hip and thigh are lightly worn. The horn and tip of tail are sharp and nearly complete.

ABOUT UNCIRCULATED (AU-50)

Traces of mint luster still show.

OBVERSE: Traces of wear show on hair above and to left of forehead, and at the cheekbone.

REVERSE: Traces of wear show on tail, hip and hair above and around the horn.

CHOICE ABOUT UNCIRCULATED (AU-55)

Half of the mint luster is still present.

OBVERSE: Only a trace of wear shows on high point of cheek.

REVERSE: A trace of wear shows on the hip.

The Complete Guide to Buffalo Nickels

VERY CHOICE ABOUT UNCIRCULATED
(AU-58)

Has some signs of abrasion: high points of Indian's cheek; hip bone, flank. Shallow or weak spots in the relief are usually caused by improper striking and not wear.

UNCIRCULATED
(MS-60)

A strictly Uncirculated coin with no trace of wear, but with blemishes more obvious than for MS-63. May lack full mint luster and surface[s] may be dull or spotted.

[CHOICE] UNCIRCULATED
(MS-63)

A mint state coin with attractive mint luster, but noticeable detracting contact marks or minor blemishes.

[GEM] UNCIRCULATED
(MS-65)

No trace of wear; nearly as perfect as MS-67 except for some small weakness or blemish. Has full mint luster but may be unevenly toned or lightly finger-marked. A few barely noticeable nicks or marks may be present.

[SUPERB GEM] UNCIRCULATED
(MS-67)

Virtually flawless but with very minor imperfections.

The following photographs features Buffalo Nickels displaying strikes of varying quality. Note that all these coins are mint state. While they exhibit no wear, they may be greatly lacking in detail.

1913-S Type 2
Weakly struck obverse (especially between 2 and 3 o' clock and at date). Rear right leg lacks detail.

1913-S Type 2
Sharply struck example of first year of issue.

1918/7-D
Softly struck in center of obverse and reverse. Note lack of buffalo's shoulder detail.

1921-S
Softly struck around periphery of both sides. Note lack of full horn on buffalo.

1923-S
Sharply struck both sides.

1923-S
Weakly struck reverse.

1925-S (?)
Weakly struck overall. In particular, note date,
central obverse, head and tail of buffalo.
Mintmark is also unclear due to erosion of die.

1935-S
Extremely weak strike on both sides. This coin was struck from
dies set too far apart. This can occur when the press is being
started or stopped and is not at full stroke. *(Bill Fivaz)*

Wear first appears on the bison's hipbone and
the raised flank directly beneath it. *(Fivaz)*

Estimating Rarity

Two factors go into determining the rarity of any given date and mint combination in a particular grade. The first of these is the coin's original mintage; the second is the percentage of this mintage that survives. The role that these both play in establishing rarity is obvious.

Logic suggests that coins supposedly common should be found with some frequency. Veterans of this hobby know that logic does not always dominate the coin market. The popularity of a series such as Buffalo Nickels may rise and fall in irregular cycles. The effect that such cycles have on prices may influence holders of these coins to either offer their collections for sale or withhold them in anticipation of better prices in the future. No one wants to sell his or her coins at a loss, and many collectors will hold on to their coins for years awaiting some upward price movement before selling.

A decline in the overall number of coin collectors since the 1960s has held down the prices of certain dates in the lower grades. This trend has primarily affected the scarcer dates in grades Good through Fine, though its influence may also be felt for some of the more common coins in grades Fine through About Uncirculated. While Buffalo Nickels continue to be bought and sold on a regular basis, many pieces in this series have become scarcer in recent years than their actual numbers would warrant, due to continued static prices. Key and semi-key dates are under almost continual upward price pressure in grades VF and higher and are thus largely immune to this phenomenon.

The Rarity Ratings are defined as follows:

R1 - Common: Available at any coin show.

R2 - A better date: Available at some small shows and all larger ones.

R3 - A tough date: Available only at larger shows.

R4 - Scarce: May not be available at larger shows.

R5 - Very scarce: Only a few will be available in a year's time.

R6 - Extremely scarce: Seldom available.

R7 - Rare: Usually placed privately or sold through a major auction.

A complete listing of the Rarity Ratings for each date/mint in various grades may be found in Table 2, Appendix B (page 189) of this book.

CHAPTER 6

Date &
Mint Analysis

GUIDE TO USING THIS ANALYSIS:

1. "Ranking" refers to the placement of that particular date/mint combination's mintage or certified population within the overall series from lowest mintage to highest. In other words, the date/mint with the lowest mintage is ranked 1/64, while the issue with the highest mintage is 64/64. The date with the lowest certified mint state population is 1/64, and the one having the highest certified population is 64/64.

2. "B" numbers are taken from *Walter Breen's Complete Encyclopedia of United States and Colonial Coins*.

3. "DDO, DDR, RPM, and OMM" designations are taken from CONECA's master index.

4. "FS" numbers are taken from *The Cherrypicker's Guide to Rare Die Varieties* by Bill Fivaz and J. T. Stanton, Fourth Edition, Mike Ellis, Editor.

5. "RATINGS" are the author's rarity estimates placed on each date/mint combination as defined in Chapter 5. These figures are collected in Table 2, Appendix B.

6. "TOTAL MS PCGS/NGC" refers to the total number of mint state coins listed in the *PCGS Population Report* and the *NGC Census Report* for January 2000.

7. "VALUES" listed under 1940 are taken from the *Standard Catalogue of United States Coins and Tokens 1940*, Wayte Raymond, Editor.

8. "VALUES" listed under 1950, 1960, 1970, 1980, 1990 and 2000 are from the 4th, 13th, 23rd, 33rd, 43rd and 53rd editions of *A Guide Book of United States Coins* by R. S. Yeoman.

9. The term "choice" in reference to grading describes a coin whose numerical grade would be MS-63 or MS-64. The term "gem" refers to a coin grading MS-65 or higher.

1913
Type 1

Mintage:
30,993,520
(Ranking 51/64)

Popular Varieties:

One reverse die was overly polished, resulting in a 3-1/2 leg variety on which the right foreleg is diminished (FS-014.85)

A cud die break is known that caused the bison's head to merge with the rim. This position is so commonly seen for cuds that I call it the "capped bison," for that is what it appears to be. Due to its close proximity to the rim and the resulting die weakness, the bison's head became the frequent location of such die breaks, as was the tail for the very same reason.

Rarity:

This issue is very common in grades XF-MS. Choice mint state examples are readily available, but their value is maintained through demand from type collectors. Gem pieces are somewhat more challenging to locate but may be acquired with a bit of patience. Coins in the lower circulated grades having readable dates are not common, as this shallow feature wore off quickly. Dateless coins are still identifiable by their distinctive reverse type but have little value. Original rolls may still exist for this issue, due to widespread hoarding at the time.

RATINGS: **G-VG** R2, **F** R2, **VF** R2, **XF-AU** R1, **MS60-63** R1, **MS64** R2, **MS65** R2

TOTAL MS PCGS/NGC = 8769 (Ranking 62/64)

Values:

	1940	1950	1960	1970	1980	1990	2000
G	——	.15	.40	1.15	2.50	3.25	4.50
F	——	.35	.75	2.00	4.00	4.50	6.00
XF	——	——	1.25	4.50	10.00	12.00	12.00
MS60	.25	.75	3.00	11.00	35.00	——	——
MS63	——	——	——	——	——	80.00	45.00

Comments:

This issue is usually well struck, though the obverse rim and LIBERTY are sometimes indistinct. The luster is typically quite brilliant, though this is may be muted by the toning seen on so many examples. The fields of all Type 1 nickels are textured as on the original models, and this often gives the luster a shimmering quality, particularly on coins struck from fresh dies. In fact, first strikes from unworn dies are easily mistaken for proofs and vice versa. See Chapter 7 for distinguishing characteristics.

Many pieces were saved as the first year of issue. Those held by the general public are often found cleaned or otherwise mishandled.

Be on the lookout for examples having no designer's initial F below the date. These may be pattern coins and can exist with either a flat-top or round-top 3 in the date. A few of these rare and valuable coins may remain undetected in collections or in dealers' stocks.

FS-014.85
(Fivaz/Stanton)

1913-D
TYPE 1

Mintage:
5,337,000
(Ranking 16/64)

Popular Varieties:

Minor doubling of the Indian's profile and the date is common. This is mechanical or strike doubling rather than a doubled die, and it carries no premium value.

Also known for this date is a "two-feathers" variety (FS-014.861) on which the Indian's shallow, innermost feather has been removed from the die through heavy polishing. This action was usually taken in response to a die clash. When the dies struck one another without a planchet between them, each received an inverted impression of the other. These ghost-like lines then appeared on each coin made from the dies until a workman removed the marks with an abrasive. Two-feathers varieties are known for several dates and are becoming increasingly popular.

Mechanical, machine or strike doubling.
(Bill Fivaz/J.T. Stanton)

Rarity:

This coin is similar to its P-Mint counterpart, with choice mint state pieces being only slightly less common. Gems are available, although most seen are toned rather than fully brilliant. Original rolls may still exist, but this is becoming increasingly unlikely.

RATINGS: G-VG R2, F R2, VF R2, XF-AU R2, MS60-63 R2, MS64 R2, MS65 R3
TOTAL MS PCGS/NGC = 2288 (Ranking 57/64)

Values:

	1940	1950	1960	1970	1980	1990	2000
G	——		1.00	3.25	5.50	6.25	8.00
F	——		2.00	6.00	7.00	8.75	10.00
XF	——	——	4.00	10.00	14.00	22.50	23.00
MS60	1.50	4.50	9.00	24.00	42.50	——	——
MS63	——	——	——	——	——	125.00	67.00

Comments:

Unlike its brothers from the east and west coasts, the Denver Mint Type 1 nickel is almost always well struck. In fact, it often makes a far superior example for a type set. These coins are typically quite lustrous, with the textured surfaces unique to the Type 1 nickels. Golden toning, sometimes accompanied by peripheral, rainbow coloring, is not unusual for this issue, which was saved in large numbers by the non-numismatic public.

The D mintmark is small and of the type first used on the cents of 1911. It remained in use as late as 1917.

1913-S
TYPE 1

Mintage:
2,105,000
(Ranking 7/64)

Popular Varieties:

A few repunched mintmark varieties are reported.

Clashed dies are common, part of E PLURIBUS UNUM appearing inverted under the Indian's chin. This is the so-called "chin whiskers" or "lettered chin" variety, and it occurs for many date/mint issues within this series.

Also known is a two-feathers variety in which the shallow, innermost feather in the Indian's hair has been polished out of the die.

The doubled profile that results from mechanical or strike doubling is particularly common with this issue and has no added value.

Two feathers.
(Norm Talbert)

Rarity:

1913-S Type 1 nickels are usually available in XF-AU and in the lower mint state grades. Choice and gem examples are scarce; the latter may be considered rare, due to the frequency of poorly struck coins.

RATINGS: G-VG R3, **F** R3, **VF** R2, **XF-AU** R2, **MS60-63** R2, **MS64** R3, **MS65** R4

TOTAL MS PCGS/NGC = 1532 (Ranking 44/64)

Values:

	1940	1950	1960	1970	1980	1990	2000
G	——	.75	2.25	4.75	6.25	9.50	12.00
F	——	1.75	5.50	8.50	10.00	16.00	19.00
XF	——	——	9.00	15.00	20.00	40.00	42.00
MS60	2.50	10.00	17.50	37.50	60.00	——	——
MS63	——	——	——	——	——	175.00	110.00

Comments:

The quality of strike is usually a make-or-break factor in locating a nice example of this issue. Central details are well struck, but peripheral elements such as the mintmark are often indistinct. A flattened portion of the rim extending from two o'clock to four o'clock obverse and visible on the corresponding portion of the reverse is common to this date.

1913-S Type 1 nickels typically have good to excellent luster. The poorly struck pieces may have very brilliant and satiny surfaces that often assist them in obtaining high certified grades, while the better struck pieces are usually characterized by more subdued luster.

The S mintmark is of the type first used for the Lincoln Cents of 1909. It remained in use for this and other denominations as late as 1917. This punch is readily identified by a small depression within the upper serif, and it serves as a good deterrent to added mintmarks, since these are usually taken from more common coins of the 1930s and are different in style.

1913
TYPE 2

Mintage:
29,858,700
(Ranking 50/64)

Popular Varieties:

Significant obverse die doubling is known and is most visible in the date (DDO-1, FS-014.8). This obverse die may have been used with a Type 1 reverse as well, but it remains unconfirmed.

There is a very distinct doubled-die reverse variety affecting the value FIVE CENTS (FS-014.86)

A small cud die break at the tail is also known.

Rarity:

This issue is very common in XF-MS, although slightly less so than for Type 1. Choice and gem pieces may be found but are far scarcer than for the earlier type. G-VG pieces are scarce, F-VF a little less so. Original rolls may still exist.

RATINGS: G-VG R2, **F** R2, **VF** R2, **XF-AU** R2, **MS60-63** R2, **MS64** R3, **MS65** R4

TOTAL MS PCGS/NGC = 1892 (Ranking 50/64)

Values:

	1940	1950	1960	1970	1980	1990	2000
G	——	.20	.35	1.50	3.00	3.00	4.75
F	——	.45	.85	3.25	4.75	4.25	7.50
XF	——	——	1.50	5.25	9.00	13.00	12.00
MS60	.75	1.50	3.50	12.50	30.00	——	——
MS63	——	——	——	——	——	80.00	50.00

Comments:

The changeover to the Type 2 reverse was ordered on May 6, and coinage of the revised nickels commenced four days later.[1]

The placing of the value FIVE CENTS within an exergue was accompanied by a smoothing of the textured fields. As a result, the luster is more satiny than the shimmering luster characteristic of Type 1 nickels. As the dies wore, of course, this satiny finish became increasingly frosty due to the presence of metal flow lines in the dies. Most 1913 Type 2 nickels have good to excellent luster, but they're less often seen with the golden and rainbow toning so often seen on the Type 1 edition.

The strike of this issue is not equal to that of Type 1 pieces, the exception being that Type 2 coins usually have more clearly defined rims at the cost of slightly weaker centers (Indian's hair knot, bison's shoulder).

Doubled-die reverse
(Fivaz/Stanton)

1913-D
TYPE 2

Mintage:
4,156,000
(Ranking 11/64)

Popular Varieties:

None are reported.

Rarity: 1913-D Type 2 nickels are scarce in all grades, but this is particularly true of the lower grades of G-F due to this coin's shallow date. This fact is reflected in the disproportionately small spread in value between G and XF.

RATINGS: G-VG R3, **F** R3, **VF** R3, **XF-AU** R3, **MS60-63** R3, **MS64** R3, **MS65** R4

TOTAL MS PCGS/NGC = 757 (Ranking 22/64)

Values:

	1940	1950	1960	1970	1980	1990	2000
G	——	.75	8.00	17.50	25.00	40.00	40.00
F	——	3.50	15.00	27.50	35.00	55.00	60.00
XF	——	——	22.50	42.00	55.00	100.00	80.00
MS60	2.00	11.00	37.50	76.50	100.00	——	——
MS63	——	——	——	——	——	325.00	250.00

Comments: The strike is again superior to that of Philadelphia and San Francisco coins. Unlike Type 1 pieces, these were not hoarded to any great extent.

This issue has the smooth fields typical of all later Buffalo Nickels, as this reflected a deliberate change made by U. S. Mint Chief Engraver Charles Barber. The luster of these coins is usually good but not outstanding.

1913-S
TYPE 2

Mintage:
1,209,000
(Ranking 3/64)

Popular Varieties:

Two repunched mintmark varieties are reported. Die clash marks are also common for this date, as is the case for most issues in the series. A small cud die break may be found at the bison's head connecting it to the rim. Another more dramatic one obliterated most of the word FIVE, as the exergue partially broke away from the die.

Rarity:

In all grades this date is scarcer than its D-Mint counterpart, particularly with a full date and LIBERTY. Choice pieces are scarce, gems truly rare.

RATINGS: G-VG R4, **F** R4, **VF** R3, **XF-AU** R3, **MS60-63** R4, **MS64** R4, **MS65** R5

TOTAL MS PCGS/NGC = 838 (Ranking 28/64)

Values:

	1940	1950	1960	1970	1980	1990	2000
G	——	4.50	12.50	29.00	41.00	65.00	90.00
F	——	8.50	27.50	46.00	62.50	115.00	155.00
XF	——	——	45.00	70.00	90.00	200.00	240.00
MS60	7.50	25.00	70.00	120.00	175.00	——	——
MS63	——	——	——	——	——	550.00	500.00

Comments:

The strike on this issue is usually worse than for Type 1. Such weakness is most evident in the legend LIBERTY and in the date. This greatly decreases the availability of desirable specimens. The piece illustrated possesses a good strike. For an example of a weakly struck specimen, see Chapter 5.

Like the Type 1 nickels, the most lustrous examples are usually the poorly struck ones. This issue has the smoothened fields associated with all later dates, rather than the textured fields characteristic of Type 1 nickels.

This is a date frequently seen with strong clash marks. While not affecting the coin's grade, this feature may reduce its appeal for some buyers.

1914

Mintage:
20,665,738
(Ranking 44/64)

Popular Varieties:

A 1914/3 overdate is the most exciting variety for this date.

Also known is a moderate sized cud break affecting the value FIVE CENTS.

Rarity:

1914-P is slightly scarce but available in all grades G through mint state. Choice and gem pieces can be had for a price.

RATINGS: G-VG R2, **F** R2, **VF** R2, **XF-AU** R2, **MS60-63** R2, **MS64** R2, **MS65** R3

TOTAL MS PCGS/NGC = 1378 (Ranking 41/64)

Values:

	1940	1950	1960	1970	1980	1990	2000
G	——	.25	.50	1.50	3.75	3.75	6.50
F	——	.60	1.75	3.25	5.75	5.75	9.00
XF	——	——	3.00	8.75	13.50	15.00	18.00
MS60	1.50	3.00	6.00	23.00	35.00	——	——
MS63	——	——	——	——	——	300.00	70.00

Comments:

This issue is usually found well struck and with good to excellent luster. This luster ranges from satiny to frosty, depending on the condition of the dies. Fresh dies would briefly produce somewhat prooflike coins, but they quickly lost their hard surface and began to generate coins having satiny, shimmering luster. As the dies wore and developed ridgelike flowlines, the result would be coins having frosty, textured luster. This is the die state most often seen for Buffalo Nickels of this or any date, as the dies were typically used until they failed completely.

The date 1914 is in higher relief than on the 1913 nickels, evidence that the Mint was already aware of that feature's inclination to wear. Walter Breen noted that this only subjected the date to greater exposure and thus more rapid wear, but I believe it may have prolonged the date's visibility by a few years. Sadly, by the time worn examples of this issue became desirable to collectors, most had already been rendered dateless.

1914/3

Earliest die state. Note doubling on date and ribbon.
(Photos courtesy Fivaz/Stanton)

Mintage:

(Included with 1914)

Rarity: Not yet established.

TOTAL MS PCGS/NGC = 25

TOTAL CIRCULATED PCGS/NGC = 42

Comments: The amazing thing about this variety is that it took so long to uncover. While certainly not as distinct as the 1918/7-D overdate, a sharp-eyed numismatist should have noticed it decades ago. In fact, the first example of this variety was not found until 1996. Its discoverer was R. A. Medina, who submitted his coin to Buffalo Nickel specialist Bill Fivaz as his entry in a contest initiated by Fivaz and sponsored through *CONECA*.

I was among the persons asked to examine this coin. Given the somewhat worn state of the dies, I hesitated to declare it a new overdate, though it strongly suggested one. I wanted to see a sharper impression from this die, but it was not until later in the year that a more distinctive example was found by Roger Alexander. It was then confirmed as an overdate by Bill Fivaz, and I agreed that the Alexander specimen was conclusive. It was my pleasure to attribute it as FS-014.87 on behalf of Numismatic Guaranty Corporation, which became the first company to certify this variety.

Since that time, two and possibly three obverse dies have been found with the overdate feature. This suggests that the dual-dating occurred during the creation of a working hub that then transferred this feature to each working die made from it. This explains both the appearance of several working dies displaying the overdate and also the shallowness of the undertype date. As with any transfer process, the image erodes somewhat as it is copied, and the overdates seen on each coin are thus third-generation copies.

The most common of the overdate varieties shows a series of horizontal die scratches above the date, perhaps the result of attempting to remove the underlying numeral 3. It is seen both with and without die-clash marks on either side. Another variety, less often seen, has similar die scratches running nearly parallel to the diagonal of numeral 4 and just to the left of it. On this variety, the underlying 3 is not as distinct.

Though very popular with Buffalo Nickel specialists, it remains to be seen whether this variety will enjoy widespread recognition. Each of the major grading services does certify these coins, but the shallowness of the underlying 3, even on early-die-state coins, makes this variety a bit hard to discern. When the die is worn, which seems to be the case with most examples seen, it takes someone already familiar with this variety's features to attribute it accurately. Collectors will probably always favor the 1918/7-D overdate, both for its long track record and for its more distinctive appearance, but the 1914/3-P nickel is definitely a part of this popular series.

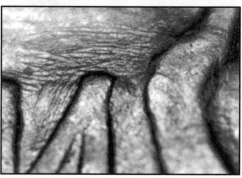

There are serveral varieties and die states of the 1914/3 overdate.
(Fivaz)

1914-D

Mintage:
3,912,000
(Ranking 10/64)

Popular Varieties:

At least one coin has been found that's suggestive of a 1914/3 overdate, but no example seen thus far is sharp enough to confirm the variety. Since the overdate feature is believed to have been in the working hub, it is possible that a working die taken from this hub may have been shipped to the Denver Mint.

A few coins may be found with minor obverse die cracks in LIBERTY and above the knot in the Indian's braid. Cracked dies seem to have been a particular problem at the Denver Mint for this and other coin types during the 1910s and early '20s.

Rarity:

Examples are quite difficult to locate in circulated grades, and problem-free coins are scarce. Choice and gem pieces are scarce but available for a price.

RATINGS: G-VG R3, **F** R3, **VF** R3, **XF-AU** R3, **MS60-63** R3, **MS64** R3, **MS65** R4

TOTAL MS PCGS/NGC = 826 (Ranking 27/64)

Values:

	1940	1950	1960	1970	1980	1990	2000
G	——	1.50	7.50	16.00	19.50	30.00	35.00
F	——	3.00	14.00	27.50	33.50	45.00	60.00
XF	——	——	22.50	50.00	57.50	100.00	120.00
MS60	2.50	15.00	40.00	115.00	150.00	——	——
MS63	——	——	——	——	——	425.00	325.00

Comments:

Despite the claims of others to the contrary, the author has found 1914-D to be generally well struck. Even so, the shallowness of the date on all 1913-1918 nickels makes these coins scarce in the lower grades with full dates. 1914-D is particularly notable for this problem.

Most 1914-D nickels have indifferent luster, though nice examples can be found. The Denver Mint frequently used its dies long after they became worn, and both flowlines and cracks are typical of its products from the mid-1910s through the mid-1920s.

1914-S

Mintage:
3,470,000
(Ranking 9/64)

Popular Varieties:

A 1914/3 overdate is the most desirable variety for this date, though it's challenging to detect.

Rarity:

1914-S is far more available in grades VF through choice mint state than might be expected for a low mintage date. Even gems are not especially rare.

RATINGS: **G-VG** R3, **F** R2, **VF** R2, **XF-AU** R2, **MS60-63** R2, **MS64** R3, **MS65** R4

Total MS PCGS/NGC = 1198 (Ranking 39/64)

Values:

	1940	1950	1960	1970	1980	1990	2000
G	——	.45	1.85	3.50	4.50	4.50	8.00
F	——	1.25	5.00	9.00	8.00	9.00	13.00
XF	——	——	16.00	22.50	19.00	37.50	37.50
MS60	2.50	13.50	35.00	67.50	90.00	——	——
MS63	——	——	——	——	——	250.00	350.00

Comments: The strike varies widely. Both mushy and well struck pieces are common; the former are often semi-prooflike. One of the peculiarities of this and other coin types is that the most fully struck examples have just so-so luster, while the most dazzling pieces are usually a bit soft in places. When the dies were not set closely enough, the result was often a coin with ill-defined highpoints but brilliant, very smooth surfaces. What one is seeing in such coins is the original surface of the unstruck planchets. These were cleaned and buffed to a bright finish that was typically altered by the compression of the dies. Where the dies failed to fully compress that surface, the coin retained the planchet's distinctive quality.

1914/3-S

Mintage:
(Included with 1914-S)

(Nick Ciancio)

Rarity: Not yet established.

TOTAL MS NGC = 5

TOTAL CIRCULATED NGC = 11

Comments: Tom DeLorey turned up the first example of this variety a year or so after the Philadelphia Mint overdate was found, and his discovery was confirmed by Bill Fivaz and J. T. Stanton. The existence of this overdate from another mint had been projected, since more than one working die was already known for the 1914/3-P. This pointed to the overdating having occurred at the hub-manufacturing stage, and thus multiple obverse working dies were created. These then could have been either used at Philadelphia, where they were made, or shipped to the other mints at Denver and San Francisco.

While the P-Mint coins are difficult to identify, the S-Mint edition is extremely so. The horizontal top of numeral 3 is just barely evident on even the sharpest, early-die-state specimens. As the attributor for NGC, I've examined several dozen coins submitted as this variety and have had to reject the majority, even when some diagnostic features of the overdate dies were evident. This is because the overdate itself was obscured through either wear on the die or wear on the coin.

One feature that seems to be present on each 1914/3-S seen thus far is a die crack on its reverse. Bill Fivaz reports that there are in fact two reverse dies for this variety, both having distinctive cracks. On the more often seen variety, this crack winds along the upper edge of the exergue into which the value FIVE CENTS is placed. Another way of saying this is that the crack runs along the bottom of the plain on which the bison stands. The crack has a slight peak to it as it passes over letter V in FIVE. Other cracks seen on this die include a prominent one connecting the bison's forehead to the rim and two lesser ones connecting each of the Indian's long feathers to the rim.

On the second reverse die, a crack runs from the rim between letter F of FIVE and the beginning of the exergue, jogs upward over the left side of letter I, continues over the right side of the left diagonal of letter V and then terminates at the top of the exergue directly above letter C in CENTS. There are no other cracks noted in this die, but the mintmark is embedded in letter C at its 7 o'clock position.

1914/3-S: Close-up of overdate
(Ciancio)

I must caution, however, that the presence of these features is not conclusive proof of an overdate. Similar cracks can appear on other dies, and the reverse die used to coin the overdate may have been paired at some point with a different obverse.

Since attribution of this variety is so challenging, not all grading services recognize it. That's why the certified population data above includes only the NGC totals. Among the obstacles in this variety's gaining recognition is that at least one example I've seen had a fine die crack running exactly where the top of the 3 was, and this may cause many people to dismiss the apparent overdate as simply a crack. Careful examination under a microscope, however, proved that both the overdate and the crack were present on this specimen.

Like the 1914/3-P, the overall popularity of this variety is hindered by the difficulty in attributing it accurately. Specialists in this series will certainly seek it out for years to come, but I suspect that, despite its greater rarity, it will prove less popular than both the 1918/7-D and 1914/3-P varieties.

1915

Mintage:
20,987,270
(Ranking 45/64)

Popular Varieties:

A doubled-die obverse is most evident along the Indian's face and at the date (DDO-1, FS-014.9).

A two-feathers variety exists for this date as well (FS-014.91)

Rarity:

1915 is more elusive than most other P-Mint nickels in the lower circulated grades; only 1914 and 1918 are scarcer. Examples are relatively common in grades XF-MS64. Gems are challenging to locate but can be found.

RATINGS: G-VG R2, **F** R2, **VF** R2, **XF-AU** R2, **MS60-63** R2, **MS64** R2, **MS65** R3

TOTAL MS PCGS/NGC = 1603 (Ranking 47/64)

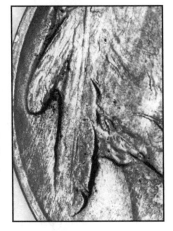

Two-feathers
(Talbert)

Values:

	1940	1950	1960	1970	1980	1990	2000
G	——	.25	.45	1.10	1.75	1.75	4.00
F	——	.60	1.50	3.00	3.25	3.75	6.25
XF	——	——	3.50	10.00	11.50	12.50	14.00
MS60	2.00	3.50	7.50	22.50	35.00	——	——
MS63	——	——	——	——	——	125.00	65.00

Comments: 1915-P nickels are among the most sharply struck coins in the series. There are many currency strikes that have been submitted to grading services by hopeful collectors and dealers who believed them to be proofs. The fact that the proofs are not so obviously different from non-proofs makes this a recurring problem.

Strike doubling
(Talbert)

The most sharply struck examples typically have the satiny luster associated with proofs, and these may have been coined with recently retired proof dies. As the dies wore, the luster they produced became more frosty and textured, yet most 1915-P nickels, whatever their die state, have outstanding luster and are very pretty coins. Though a bit more expensive than most other P-Mint nickels, this date makes an excellent type coin.

1915-D

Mintage:
7,569,000
(Ranking 28/64)

Popular Varieties:

One variety features a very distinct repunching of the mintmark (RPM-1, FS-015). Another less spectacular repunched mintmark is also reported.

A rotated reverse has been observed for this date, though such anomalies don't seem to hold much interest for collectors. Technically, it was the obverse die that rotated in the press, since Buffalo Nickels were coined with the obverse die in the lower or anvil position. Had the reverse die become loose, it would have most likely fallen from the press!

Rarity:

This date is moderately scarce in grades F through mint state, although certainly not in the same league as later D-Mint coins dated 1917-25. Gems are rare.

RATINGS: G-VG R2, **F** R3, **VF** R2, **XF-AU** R3, **MS60-63** R3, **MS64** R3, **MS65** R4

TOTAL MS PCGS/NGC = 689 (Ranking 17/64)

Values:

	1940	1950	1960	1970	1980	1990	2000
G	——	.75	1.50	4.25	5.50	6.50	9.00
F	——	2.00	5.00	10.50	11.25	15.00	22.00
XF	——	——	12.50	24.00	25.00	55.00	55.00
MS60	3.50	15.00	27.50	65.00	90.00	——	——
MS63	——	——	——	——	——	275.00	300.00

Comments:

This is the first date from the Denver Mint in which weakness of strike becomes a factor. Though not extreme, it may be evident in the central obverse and the bison's head, shoulders and tail. Well struck examples do exist and are worth the wait.

The typical 1915-D nickel has just average luster. A fairly high percentage of the surviving mint state coins show light to medium toning that is not particularly attractive. Patience will be required to find an appealing example of this issue.

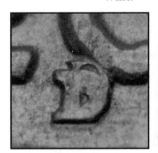

RPM-1
(Fivaz/Stanton)

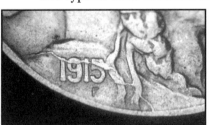

Dramatic die crack through date
(Fivaz/Stanton)

1915-S

Mintage:
1,505,000
(Ranking 5/64)

Popular Varieties:

A triple-punched mintmark is one of the most distinctive such varieties in this series (FS-015.5). Another S/S/S variety is not quite as dramatic (FS-015.6).

Minor obverse mechanical doubling, as well as clash marks on both obverse and reverse, are not unusual for this date. Neither phenomenon provides any additional value.

S/S/S. FS-015.5
(Fivaz/Stanton)

Rarity:

This is perhaps the first date in the series that will be truly difficult to locate. Although striking quality varies from mediocre to excellent, the actual number of coins that appear in all grades combined is limited. Most seen are AG-VG, with F following. Other grades are scarce, while choice and gem examples are genuinely rare.

RATINGS: G-VG R2, **F** R3, **VF** R4, **XF-AU** R4,
MS60-63 R3, **MS64** R3, **MS65** R4

TOTAL MS PCGS/NGC = 611 (Ranking 15/64)

Values:

	1940	1950	1960	1970	1980	1990	2000
G	——	.75	3.00	7.25	8.00	10.00	14.00
F	——	1.75	7.50	16.00	22.50	20.00	45.00
XF	——	——	17.50	44.00	52.50	100.00	150.00
MS60	2.00	13.50	35.00	130.00	165.00	——	——
MS63	——	——	——	——	——	600.00	750.00

Comments: 1915-S nickels may be found quite well struck with the exception of LIBERTY. More common, however, are poorly struck pieces. The latter are sometimes semi-prooflike, as the weak strike failed to fully reshape the planchet and thereby change its texture. Such brilliance may also result from overpolishing the dies in an attempt to remove the all-too-common clash marks.

As with 1915-D, there seem to be quite a number of toned examples, with this toning rarely being attractive. Dull, monochromatic toning of brownish gold is typical. There's no point in attempting to remove this toning, as the underlying luster has probably already been impaired.

The existence of numerous 1915-S nickels having extremely sharp strikes has led to speculation that proof dies were used to produce those coins. There are instances known in other coin series of retired proof dies being placed into general service, so this is not as far-fetched as it may seem. Of course, there's really little difference between a proof die and a regular die that's unworn, as both are capable of producing a sharp impression. It's likely that at least one press run of 1915-S nickels enjoyed a fresh pair of dies set closely together. This would result in very well struck examples. It's interesting to note that there are also many 1915-S Lincoln Cents having similarly sharp strikes.

1916

Mintage:
63,498,066
(Ranking 62/64)

Popular Varieties:

The 1916/1916 doubled-die obverse is one of the most desirable varieties in this or any series (FS-016). There are also pieces having a slightly doubled profile on the Indian as the result of mechanical or strike doubling. These are not true varieties, as they don't represent a feature of the die itself, and they carry little if any premium.

Also of interest is the variety without the designer's initial F. This was caused by excessive polishing of the die, probably performed in an attempt to remove clash marks (FS-016.3). One intriguing possibility that has not been explored by numismatists is that this variety may have resulted from efforts to remove the doubled image of FS-016. A comparison of both varieties might turn up some common features such as unique die cracks or polishing lines.

Finally, Norm Talbert reports that a two-feathers variety exists for this date, though it has not yet received a Cherrypicker number.

Rarity:

Coins from the normal dies are common in all grades including gem. Original rolls may still exist.

RATINGS: **G-VG** R1, **F** R1, **VF** R2, **XF-AU** R2, **MS60-63** R2, **MS64** R2, **MS65** R3

TOTAL MS PCGS/NGC = 1976 (Ranking 52/64)

Values:

	1940	1950	1960	1970	1980	1990	2000
G	——	.15	.20	.50	.75	.75	1.25
F	——	.40	1.00	1.50	1.75	1.75	2.00
XF	——	——	2.50	4.50	6.50	5.00	7.00
MS60	.75	2.25	6.00	16.50	27.50	——	——
MS63	——	——	——	——	——	90.00	60.00

Comments:

The quality of strike varies widely for 1916-P nickels. There are no really bad ones, though a number of pieces will show distinctive flatness in the central portion of the Indian's portrait. This affects the hair braid in particular. This same peculiarity is common to many 1918-P nickels.

Fully struck, highly lustrous examples are easy enough to find with a bit of shopping, and 1916-P is another issue that makes for a nice type coin. The luster of these coins is rarely satiny. More typical is very bright frostiness throughout.

The Mint finally addressed some of the Buffalo Nickel's basic deficiencies beginning this year. A new obverse hub was used exclusively for this and all subsequent dates. The word LIBERTY was more deeply incised, eliminating its tendency to blend with the coin's field. Walter Breen and others have written that further changes were made to the Indian's profile, particularly with respect to lengthening his nose. I've been unable to discern such changes, and the readers may decide for themselves.

1916
Doubled-Die Obverse

Mintage:
(Included with 1916)

Rarity: Mint state examples of this variety are extremely rare and number fewer than ten. Circulated pieces, while still rare, are more available and bring the total population to perhaps 100-150.

TOTAL MS PCGS/NGC = 7

TOTAL CIRCULATED PCGS/NGC = 91

Values:

	1980	1990	2000
G	———	600	1,700
F	———	1,250	5,000
XF	400	2,700	10,000
MS60	750	———	———
MS63	———	———	40,000

Comments: Though it's now well known and highly sought, this variety remains elusive. The values listed above give a clear indication of just how desirable this issue is to collectors. While it's still not included in albums for the series, demand is very strong. Dateless pieces may be identified by the extra thickness of the Indian's hair ribbon, but these would be worth far less than distinct examples.

The first published report of this variety (B-2599, FS-016) appeared in *The Numismatic Scrapbook Magazine* for July 1962, when an example was submitted by Herbert S. Perlin of Pomona, California. Knowledge of it, however, was not widespread until the mid-1970s. Not until it was described and illustrated in the September 1976 issue of the *Coin Dealer Newsletter Monthly Summary* did this coin gain proper recognition. It appeared shortly thereafter in the Red Book (*A Guide Book of United States Coins*, by R. S. Yeoman), and it's been a perennial favorite ever since.

1916-D

Mintage:
13,333,000
(Ranking 40/64)

Popular Varieties:

One reverse die features a misplaced mintmark that appears to be embedded in the C of CENTS.

There are rumors of several doubled-die obverses, but these are most likely examples of the mechanical or strike doubling so common to early Buffalo Nickels.

Rarity: 1916-D is not particularly scarce in all grades short of gem. The latter are rare.

RATINGS: G-VG R2, **F** R2, **VF** R2, **XF-AU** R2, **MS60-63** R2, **MS64** R3, **MS65** R5

TOTAL MS PCGS/NGC = 1071 (Ranking 34/64)

Values:

	1940	1950	1960	1970	1980	1990	2000
G	——	.35	1.00	2.85	4.50	4.50	7.00
F	——	1.00	3.00	6.50	7.50	8.00	13.00
XF	——	——	9.00	18.50	19.00	45.00	50.00
MS60	1.50	13.50	25.00	60.00	82.00	——	——
MS63	——	——	——	——	——	275.00	230.00

Comments: Although well struck pieces can be found with perseverance, most are weak in the central obverse and the bison's head and shoulder. Examples grading Good with a full date are scarce. This is true of many dates in the 1913-18 period, as their dates were quite delicately drawn.

1916-D nickels usually have good to excellent luster, though they suffer from overly worn dies. While many collectors like the very frosty, texture luster that results from eroded dies, and such coins often receive high grades from grading services, my personal preference has always been for coins that have sharp, complete details. In an ironic twist, such coins typically have muted, satiny luster.

Imbedded D

1916-S

Mintage:
11,860,000
(Ranking 38/64)

Popular Varieties:

Two similar and quite major cud die breaks are known in which part of the obverse die has broken away. A lesser cud is known at the bison's tail. Although commonly classified with error coins, this phenomenon is more correctly described as a variety. Whereas error coins are each unique, a cud will appear on every coin struck from a die possessing this defect until it is spotted and the die removed.

Rarity:

This date is slightly scarce in the lower circulated grades and rare in gem condition. Other grades are more available, VF-XF pieces being relatively common.

RATINGS: G-VG R2, **F** R2, **VF** R2, **XF-AU** R2, **MS60-63** R3, **MS64** R3, **MS65** R4

TOTAL MS PCGS/NGC = 809 (Ranking 24-25/64)

Values:

	1940	1950	1960	1970	1980	1990	2000
G	——	.35	1.00	2.25	3.00	3.00	4.00
F	——	1.00	4.00	6.00	6.00	6.00	9.00
XF	——	——	11.00	20.00	19.00	42.50	40.00
MS60	1.25	13.50	32.50	65.00	100.00	——	——
MS63	——	——	——	——	——	260.00	300.00

Comments:

Although fully struck mint state coins are difficult to locate, many circulated pieces are sharper in detail. This is simply the luck of the draw. An area of particular weakness is the tip of each feather. Some coins, even well struck pieces, display die erosion just inside the obverse and reverse borders. This appears as a thin ring of built up metal that gives the impression of a second border. While attractive to some collectors, it may be disturbing to others.

Note the strong die clash marks on the coin illustrated. The outline of the bison's back may be seen to the left of the Indian's neck, and part of E PLURIBUS UNUM appears inverted to the right of his neck ("chin whiskers"). The Indian's chin also appears below UNUM on the reverse. This problem is commonly seen on Buffalo Nickels. While clash marks may detract from a coin's appearance, they do not affect its grade.

Heavy cud at 10 o' clock
(Talbert)

1916-S nickels typically have very nice luster. Well struck examples are likely to be frosty or satiny, while the softer ones may have very a bright and metallic surface.

1917

Mintage:
51,424,019
(Ranking 58/64)

Popular Varieties:

The prominent doubled-die reverse for this date is very highly sought (DDR-1, FS-016.4). The doubling is most evident in the legend E PLURIBUS UNUM. A lesser doubled-die variety turned up while collectors and dealers were searching for the big one (DDR-2, FS-016.41). Its value is significantly lower than for the primary variety.

A two-feathers variety exists for this issue (FS-016.411).

DDR-1
(Fivaz/Stanton)

DDR-1
(Fivaz/Stanton)

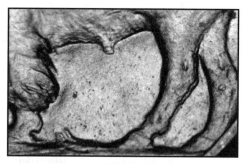

DDR-1
(Fivaz/Stanton)

Rarity:

1917-P is fairly common in all grades short of the gem level (MS-65 and higher). Original rolls may yet exist.

RATINGS: G-VG R1, **F** R1, **VF** R2, **XF-AU** R2, **MS60-63** R2, **MS64** R2, **MS65** R4

TOTAL MS PCGS/NGC = 1037 (Ranking 33/64)

Values:

	1940	1950	1960	1970	1980	1990	2000
G	——	.15	.25	.45	.85	.85	1.25
F	——	.35	.65	1.30	1.90	1.90	2.50
XF	——	——	1.50	5.00	10.00	8.00	10.00
MS60	.75	2.50	6.50	18.00	35.00	——	——
MS63	——	——	——	——	——	110.00	65.00

Comments: Most examples seen are very sharply struck, yet a few show evidence of heavy die erosion from extended use of the dies. The nationwide shortage of minor coins in 1917-18 probably accounts for this development, although it would be repeated with disturbing frequency in subsequent years.

1917-P nickels vary widely in the quality of their luster. The vast majority have very textured, frosty luster as a consequence of extended die usage. Earlier strikes are a bit more satiny.

Beginning this year, the obverse design was strengthened in the lines of the Indian's robe above the date. This addressed another of the deficiencies in the original models and represents a refinement to the hub of 1916.

1917-D

Mintage:
9,910,000
(Ranking 35/64)

Popular Varieties:

Vigorous polishing of a reverse die produced the 3-1/2-leg variety (FS-016.42). The popularity of such pieces is due to their association with the more dramatic 1937-D 3-leg variety.

A two-feathers variety is also known (FS-016.43).

A new mintmark style was introduced this year, and 1917-D nickels may be found with either the old (1913-17) D or the new (1917-34) Denver mintmark. These are similar at first glance, and there doesn't seem to be any interest among collectors in obtaining both styles.

Two feathers.
(Norm Talbert)

Rarity:

1917-D is a scarce date in circulated grades VF and better. Low end mint state coins are more available than XF-AU, but both share the same problem with strike. Choice and gem pieces are rare.

RATINGS: G-VG R2, **F** R2, **VF** R3, **XF-AU** R4, **MS60-63** R3, **MS64** R3, **MS65** R4

TOTAL MS PCGS/NGC = 593 (Ranking 14/64)

Values:

	1940	1950	1960	1970	1980	1990	2000
G	——	.50	1.65	2.80	3.50	4.50	7.00
F	——	1.75	6.00	9.50	9.25	11.00	20.00
XF	——	——	20.00	40.00	45.00	85.00	85.00
MS60	3.00	20.00	42.50	80.00	140.00	——	——
MS63	——	——	——	——	——	365.00	450.00

Comments:

Nearly all examples seen suffer from poor detail definition. This is due in large part to the die erosion described for 1917-P. For the D-Mint, however, it is much more severe, extending into the recesses of the dies instead of merely affecting the fields.

Commonly seen are individual coins that have more than one kind of luster. A blend of satiny and frosty textures is typical, as eroded areas of the dies alternated with smooth ones. Repolishing of worn or clashed dies seems to have been practiced, and this can produce isolated areas of prooflike reflectivity for this and many other issues in the Buffalo Nickel series.

1917-S

Mintage:
4,193,000
(Ranking 12/64)

Popular Varieties:

A two-feathers variety exists for this date (FS-016.44). The die polishing that led to this distinctive variety was likely prompted by an attempt to remove clash marks. For more about die clashing, see Comments.

A new S mintmark punch was introduced early in this year, and examples may be found with either the old (1913-17) or new (1917-37) mintmarks. Their relative rarity remains unstudied, but collectors don't seem to care about these varieties.

Two feathers.
(Norm Talbert)

Rarity: 1917-S nickels are very scarce in all grades. Gems are particularly elusive.

RATINGS: G-VG R3, **F** R4, **VF** R4, **XF-AU** R4, **MS60-63** R3, **MS64** R3, **MS65** R4

TOTAL MS PCGS/NGC = 372 (Ranking 4/64)

Values:

	1940	1950	1960	1970	1980	1990	2000
G	——	.60	1.65	3.25	3.25	3.50	6.00
F	——	2.00	6.00	10.50	9.25	10.00	25.00
XF	——	——	25.00	42.50	45.00	70.00	110.00
MS60	3.50	25.00	60.00	120.00	175.00	——	——
MS63	——	——	——	——	——	390.00	625.00

Comments: As with 1915-S nickels, a relatively small number of coins may be found that are extremely well struck. Again, it has been suggested that these were coined from proof dies. More likely is that the dies were simply unworn and closely set within the press, the ideal situation for any coining operation but one that was seldom maintained with respect to Buffalo Nickels. Most examples of this date have strong central details but weak peripheral elements. This is enhanced by the prevalence of erosion in the die along the inner border, as described for 1916-S.

As the typical 1917-S nickel is poorly struck from worn dies, its luster will alternate between the bright, metallic sheen associated with uncompressed planchets and the frosty, textured quality of worn die steel. This date and others that are typically not well struck sometimes have an overall texture that calls to mind the appearance of liquid mercury. Again, this is simply the natural quality of the polished planchet when it is not fully compressed by the dies.

In the first edition of this book I made the observation that 1917-S nickels appeared to be undervalued in circulated grades. The coin market seems to have agreed, judging by the price advances shown between 1990 and 2000.

In the May 1945 issue of *The Numismatic Scrapbook Magazine*, J. V. Barton's letter to the editor commented on a peculiarity familiar to all collectors of Buffalo Nickels:

> Very few collectors have noticed the "Lettered Chin" or "Blanked Die" Buffalo Nickels minted at the San Francisco and Philadelphia Mints.
>
> On these nickels some of the letters of PLURIBUS appear on the obverse of the coin under the chin of the Indian. The lettering is Upside-down and in reverse, and is exactly opposite the Pluribus on the reverse of the coin. Only the first one to five letters of the Pluribus appear. Some of these coins are so well struck that this lettering can be easily seen and read without the use of a magnifying glass. A letter dated February 12th, 1944, from the Superintendent of the Philadelphia Mint, advises as follows: – "This coin apparently was struck from a 'Blanked' pair of dies, the dies having touched without a planchet between, leaving an impression of a portion of the reverse die on the highest point of the obverse die."

Reader Barton went on to list the various dates known by him to have lettered chins, or "chin whiskers," as they've also been called: 1913-S Type 1, 1913-S Type 2, 1914, 1914-S, 1916-S, 1917-S, 1918-S, 1919-S, 1920, 1920-S, 1921, 1923-S, 1924-S, 1925-S, 1927-S, 1928-S and 1929-S. Other dates may also turn up with this common feature.

Now known in the numismatic field as clash marks, these inverted impressions of opposing dies are commonly seen on many dates within the Buffalo Nickel series. A corresponding flattening of the legend E PLURIBUS UNUM typically accompanies the lettered chin on clashed die pairs, as this portion of the reverse die was simultaneously damaged by the Indian's chin and neck. Such coins carry no premium, though the two-feather varieties that sometimes occurred from attempts to remove clash marks are popular with collectors.

1918

Mintage:
32,086,314
(Ranking 52/64)

Popular Varieties:

One reverse die shows doubling within the Latin legend (FS-016.45). It is easily seen, despite being partially obscured by clash marks.

A two-feathers variety is also known (FS-016.46). This class of variety has been dubbed an abraded-die obverse (ADO), but it's too soon to tell whether this terminology will be widely adopted by the hobby.

Rarity:

1918 is a scarce coin in all grades F and better. Despite its high mintage, nice circulated coins are frustratingly elusive, due in part to a chronically poor strike. Mediocre mint state coins are often available, but not so gem pieces. The total certified mint state population is surprisingly low.

RATINGS: G-VG R2, **F** R3, **VF** R3, **XF-AU** R4, **MS60-63** R3, **MS64** R3, **MS65** R4

TOTAL MS PCGS/NGC = 706 (Ranking 20/64)

Values:

	1940	1950	1960	1970	1980	1990	2000
G	——	.20	.25	.50	.85	.85	1.25
F	——	.70	1.50	1.85	2.75	2.50	2.50
XF	——	——	3.00	10.75	12.50	15.00	16.00
MS60	1.50	6.00	16.50	47.50	60.00	——	——
MS63	——	——	——	——	——	180.00	125.00

Comments:

The typical 1918 nickel is quite flat in the central obverse, the knot which secures the Indian's braid having no detail at all. The corresponding portion of the reverse is similarly affected, though to a less dramatic extent. The rest of the coin will usually exhibit an adequate to good strike. Shown above is an exceptionally well struck example.

1918-P nickels exhibit luster than ranges from average to excellent. Coins struck from fresh dies tend to be satiny, while the vast majority of mint state coins are frosty and textured. The planchets used for this issue may display toning streaks from poor mixing of the alloy. The three United States Mints were individually responsible for securing their supplies of nickel blanks, alternately producing them in-house from strip or purchasing them ready-made. This irregularity of supply led to certain date/mint issues having peculiar characteristics such as the laminations that plagued the 1921-S nickels.

This high-mintage issue is inexplicably difficult to locate across all grades, the number of coins reportedly struck being at odds with this date's survival rate. Where did they all go? Bill Fivaz notes that 1918-P has more than its share of off-center examples, and such physical evidence may reflect the increase in new hires that resulted during each of the 20th Century's major wars. The quality of the coins during these difficult times always fell, as production soared and inexperienced personnel filled the places left vacant by servicemen. Is it possible that technical problems plagued the 1918-P nickels and that the published mintage figures may include many coins which ultimately had to be withheld from release? Although undocumented and inconsistent with Mint practice, this theory remains interesting food for thought.

1918-D

Mintage:
8,362,000
(Ranking 31/64)

Popular Varieties:

The 1918/7 overdate is the most valuable and desired variety in this series (B-2608, DDO-1, FS-016.5).

Other than the occasional instance of clash marks, a variety that carries no premium, there is nothing else known for this issue.

Rarity:

1918-D is scarce in all grades VF and better. Mint state coins are available with the characteristic weakness of strike. Choice and gem pieces are rare.

RATINGS: **G-VG** R2, **F** R3, **VF** R3, **XF-AU** R4, **MS60-63** R3, **MS64** R4, **MS65** R5

TOTAL MS PCGS/NGC = 500 (Ranking 11/64)

Values:

	1940	1950	1960	1970	1980	1990	2000
G	——	.55	1.45	3.00	3.50	4.50	7.00
F	——	2.00	5.50	9.00	10.00	12.00	22.00
XF	——	——	22.50	50.00	55.00	85.00	120.00
MS60	3.50	35.00	57.50	165.00	250.00	——	——
MS63	——	——	——	——	——	550.00	650.00

Comments:

The same striking problems described for 1918-P are evident here, but to a greater degree. Since the bison's horn remains fairly sharp, this deficiency shouldn't present any difficulty in grading, but it will make finding a desirable coin somewhat challenging. The example shown is exceptional.

1918-D nickels usually have luster that is just average to good. Many surviving examples are toned to varying degrees, this toning sometimes reflecting irregularities in the alloy that appear as pale, coppery streaks. When the toning is deeper, its simulates a woodgrain pattern.

As American soldiers arrived in France during the summer of 1918, they brought with them supplies of their native money, which proved to be readily accepted by the locals. One account noted that "Newspaper venders, boat ticket sellers and others who deal largely in pennies, would much rather accept an American nickel or a couple of cents than change a 5-franc note. They are readily taken where there will be a later opportunity to pass it back in change to an American customer." The account continued, "The French like the American 5-cent piece. 'Elle est jolie,' they say, comparing it with the French coin of the same denomination with a square hole in the center."[2]

1918/7-D

Note diagnostic die crack and shape of
designer's initial
(Tom Mulvaney)

Enlargement of date area
(Fivaz/Stanton)

Mintage:
Included with 1918-D

Rarity: The overdate is seldom visible below VG, which is the grade most often found. A number of coins grading VG-F may also be available at large shows, but anything in higher grades is rare. The exact number of uncirculated survivors is unknown. Accounting for possible resubmissions of the same coins to grading services, it's likely that about two dozen or so have survived.

RATINGS: **G-VG** R3, **F** R4, **VF** R4, **XF-AU** R5, **MS60-63** R6, **MS64** R7, **MS65** R8

TOTAL MS PCGS/NGC = 44

TOTAL CIRCULATED PCGS/NGC = 369

Values:

	1950	1960	1970	1980	1990	2000
G	——	45.00	150.00	165.00	415.00	350.00
F	30.00	150.00	400.00	475.00	725.00	900.00
XF	——	375.00	1,175	1,850	2,500	4,500
MS60	175.00	——	5,300	9,500	——	——
MS63	——	——	——	——	14,000	30,000

Comments: The 1918/7-D overdate certainly rivals the 1916/1916 and 1937-D 3-leg nickel for the title of most popular and highly sought variety in the series. Though discovered as long ago as 1931, it still remains scarce.

The obverse die for this variety was actually manufactured during the latter part of 1917 at the Philadelphia Mint. It was during the final quarter of each year that the Mint's engraving department began preparing dies for the new year's coinage. As described in the Comments for 1917-P, a nationwide shortage of minor coins (cents and nickels) developed during 1917-18 and led to an unprecedented output of these. It is therefore easy to understand that dies for both 1917 and 1918 would have been in preparation during the latter months of 1917 to meet both current and anticipated needs.

In sinking a working die, two or more impressions had to be taken from a working hub. Between each impression, the developing die was taken to the furnace to be annealed, or softened, since the first impression caused the metal to become work-hardened. It was then ready for another impression. Amid the haste to produce new dies, a working die that had already been impressed with a hub dated 1917 was then either inadvertently or intentionally given another impression from a hub dated 1918. The result was an overdate.

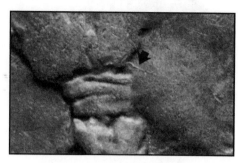

Close up of diagnostic die crack
(Fivaz/Stanton)

Considering its value, authentication is recommended for this coin. Any suspected overdate must look like the one illustrated. Genuine examples usually have a fine die crack just above the knot of the Indian's braid, though this may not be present on coins struck from the earliest state of the die. Also, the top of the 8 extends halfway up into the horizontal bar of the 7; the two "ears" of that bar show fully as well as its flat top surface, and the diagonal of the 7 underneath the 8 is straight, not curved. Another feature that may also help to distinguish worn examples of this variety is the pattern of die erosion seen in the photo. Note in particular the misshapen designer's initial **F** that has assumed the appearance of a P.

1918-S

Mintage:
4,882,000
(Ranking 14/64)

Popular Varieties:

One or more two-feathers varieties exist, though these are typically placed under a single number (FS-016.6).

One die shows an interesting crack through the date that progressed to become a retained cud.

Rarity:

Although scarce in grades VF and better, this date is more often available than 1918-D in XF-AU. Mint state coins are few, while choice and gem pieces are rare and seldom offered.

RATINGS: G-VG R2, **F** R2, **VF** R3, **XF-AU** R4, **MS60-63** R4, **MS64** R4, **MS65** R6

TOTAL MS PCGS/NGC = 404 (Ranking 6/64)

Values:

	1940	1950	1960	1970	1980	1990	2000
G	——	.55	1.45	2.75	3.00	3.50	6.00
F	——	2.00	6.00	9.00	9.50	9.50	19.00
XF	——	——	27.50	47.50	52.50	75.00	150.00
MS60	3.00	35.00	67.50	175.00	225.00	——	——
MS63	——	——	——	.	——	475.00	2,000

Comments:

The striking problem noted for 1918-P and D is much worse for 1918-S. In addition, the date is sometimes weak, especially in the first two digits. Most examples have frosty luster that is somewhat subdued. A very bright 1918-S nickel is a rarity, but then so are mint state examples of any quality.

What appears as weak striking on Buffalo Nickels and other United States coins of the 1910s and '20s is actually a combination of factors. In some instances the dies were set too far apart to make a complete impression. This was done as an economy measure to reduce wear on both the dies and press and to thus extend their useful life. Such economy was practiced even more vigorously during the 1920s, as the budgets of most governmental departments were slashed by the parsimonious Harding and Coolidge administrations.

The Buffalo Nickel was a coin of relatively high relief, and it did take quite a toll on the dies. These wore rapidly, and such erosion is often evident on the actual coins. The reverse dies in particular were used too long, as they didn't need to be discarded at the end of each calendar year. The combination of increased die-set distances and worn dies produced the mushy, disappointing coins so often seen in this series.

1919

Mintage:
60,868,000
(Ranking 60/64)

Popular Varieties:

A two-feathers variety exists for this date (FS-016.61). It is evidently unique among this class of variety in that it also lacks Fraser's initial F.

At least two prominent cud breaks are known connecting the bison's head to the rim, a common location for such die failures. Other cuds are known for this date in the area above the bison's back and rump, respectively, as are a few of varying size on the obverse.

DDO-1
(Talbert)

Two feathers. FS-016.61
(Fivaz/Stanton)

Rarity:

1919-P is common in all grades through choice mint state. Gems are not particularly scarce, assuming that one discounts the slight softness of strike characteristic of this issue. Original rolls may still exist, those this is becoming increasingly unlikely.

RATINGS: G-VG R1, **F** R1, **VF** R2, **XF-AU** R2, **MS60-63** R2, **MS64** R2, **MS65** R3

TOTAL MS PCGS/NGC = 1230 (Ranking 40/64)

Values:

	1940	1950	1960	1970	1980	1990	2000
G	——	.15	.25	.40	.65	.65	1.00
F	——	.40	.60	1.25	1.50	1.50	1.50
XF	——	——	1.75	5.50	7.50	7.50	7.50
MS60	1.00	3.25	7.50	24.00	32.50	——	——
MS63	——	——	——	——	——	85.00	75.00

Comments: Most pieces seen have a general softness of strike that is evenly distributed throughout the design. Thus, no one area can be described as being weak. When such weakness is typical of a particular date/mint combination, it's likely the result of inadequately hubbed dies. Since hundreds of working dies would have been needed to produce such a large mintage as that of the 1919-P nickels, it's not surprising that both soft and sharp coins may be found. This date is common enough that a shopper may take his or her time and select a well struck example.

This issue typically displays excellent luster that is almost always frosty and bright. Satiny examples are rare, as would be expected of a date that had such a high mintage. It's obvious that the dies were used for very long press runs, and the resulting die erosion and metal flowlines produced the frosty luster so common for 1919-P nickels.

In this and subsequent years the digits of the date are noticeably bolder. Evidently the mint was taking remedial action against the tendency of the date to wear down. By the end of 1918 this phenomenon must have been all too obvious. Alas, the effort was largely in vain. A more practical solution would have been that taken in 1925 in response to a similar situation with the Standing Liberty Quarter, that is, recessing the date within an exergue.

A single coin described as a "specimen" striking has been reported but is presently unconfirmed (see Chapter 7).

The large number of nickels and other United States coins minted in this year did not go unnoticed by the numismatic press. Though it underestimated the eventual scarcity of certain issues, this account expressed a sentiment widely held at the time:

> A glance at the table of coinage by the different mints for last year will show that "1919" will be known as a "common date" for all denominations struck at each of the three mints. The rarest coin, evidently, is the half dollar of the Philadelphia mint. But as nearly a million of these coins were struck, there is little chance of it becoming even scarce. Of the other denominations, those struck at the San Francisco and Denver mints are far less plentiful than of the Philadelphia Mint, but even so, there will be enough to meet the needs of collectors, as well as for other mortals.[3]

1919-D

Mintage:
8,006,000
(Ranking 30/64)

Popular Varieties:

A bold die break appears on some examples. If allowed to remain in the press, this die would have likely resulted in a cud. Speaking of which, at least one cud is known for both the obverse and reverse, respectively.

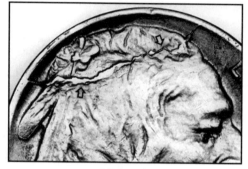

Die break
(Talbert)

Rarity:

This is a scarce coin in all grades F and better. Weak striking is a major obstacle to locating suitable specimens. 1919-D and 1920-D are ranked equally by Larry Whitlow as the two rarest D-Mint Buffalo Nickels to locate in fully struck gem condition, however, Norm Talbert considers 1927-D to be scarcer with a full strike than 1919-D.

RATINGS: G-VG R2, **F** R2, **VF** R3, **XF-AU** R4, **MS60-63** R4, **MS64** R4, **MS65** R5

TOTAL MS PCGS/NGC = 391 (Ranking 5/64)

Values:

	1940	1950	1960	1970	1980	1990	2000
G	——	.55	1.50	3.00	3.75	4.00	7.25
F	——	2.00	7.50	11.50	11.50	11.50	28.00
XF	——	——	37.50	70.00	75.00	100.00	165.00
MS60	3.50	32.50	80.00	205.00	325.00	——	——
MS63	——	——	——	——	——	650.00	900.00

Comments:

1919-D is one of the more challenging issues to locate fully struck in the period of generally weak coins that extended from 1917 through 1926. It is one of the last holes filled by a discriminating collector, regardless of whether one is collecting XF-AU or gem uncirculated.

Like 1919-P, weakness of strike is rather evenly distributed. One exception is the forepart of the bison's head, which is drastically flattened on most pieces. This will affect the grading of 1919-D nickels, as the horn is also somewhat indistinct at its tip. As noted for 1919-P, such isolated weakness may be due to deficiencies in the die itself.

1919-D nickels typically have just average to good luster. Many are toned to varying degrees, and this can range from the streaky gold "woodgrain" pattern to a dull, monochromatic film. Colorfully toned examples are quite rare.

1919-S

Mintage:
7,521,000
(Ranking 27/64)

Popular Varieties:

None are reported, though this issue is a likely candidate for a two-feathers obverse.

Rarity:

1919-S is scarce in all grades VF and better. Fully struck coins are nearly unknown.
RATINGS: G-VG R2, **F** R2, **VF** R3, **XF-AU** R4, **MS60-63** R4, **MS64** R4, **MS65** R5
TOTAL MS PCGS/NGC = 412 (Ranking 7/64)

Values:

	1940	1950	1960	1970	1980	1990	2000
G	——	.55	1.75	2.75	2.50	2.50	5.00
F	——	2.00	7.50	11.50	8.75	9.00	18.00
XF	——	——	45.00	67.50	65.00	80.00	170.00
MS60	3.50	35.00	95.00	200.00	300.00	——	——
MS63	——	——	——	——	——	525.00	950.00

Comments:

This date is notorious for being weakly struck, particularly on the reverse. Problem areas include the border, denomination, mintmark and the bison's head with its all-important horn. Mint state coins may look worn, yet lustrous. The example shown is exceptionally sharp.

1919-S nickels usually have disappointing luster. The typically seen mushy example may have the smooth, mercury-like luster so common to weakly struck nickels, but it is seldom accompanied by the brilliance often associated with such coins. Toned examples are common, and this toning is usually not attractive.

Note that the values for lower grade examples declined between 1970 and 1990 and have only recently rebounded. For an explanation of this phenomenon, see Chapter 2.

1920

Mintage:
63,093,000
(Ranking 61/64)

Popular Varieties:

A major cud variety exists dated 1920 but with the mintmark area obscured, leaving its origin unknown. This variety also displays die clash marks above the bison. Numerous other cuds are found for this date, most of them affecting all or part of the value FIVE CENTS. Being set within an exergue, this design element was particularly vulnerable to failure.

A two-feathers variety is also known for this date, though it has not yet been assigned a Cherrypicker number.

Heavy cud at 5-7 o' clock
(Talbert)

Rarity:

1920 is a fairly common date in all grades. Original rolls may yet exist, though this is becoming increasingly unlikely.

RATINGS: **G-VG** R1, **F** R1, **VF** R2, **XF-AU** R2, **MS60-63** R2, **MS64** R2, **MS65** R3

TOTAL MS PCGS/NGC = 961 (Ranking 31/64)

Values:

	1940	1950	1960	1970	1980	1990	2000
G	——	.15	.15	.40	.65	.65	1.00
F	——	.40	.75	1.15	1.50	1.50	1.50
XF	——	——	1.75	5.75	7.50	7.50	9.00
MS60	1.00	3.25	7.50	22.50	30.00	——	——
MS63	——	——	——	——	——	90.00	75.00

Comments:

Like the 1919-P nickel, this coin frequently exhibits an overall softness in strike. This is compensated by the sheer number of pieces that may be found in mint state grades, as these provide a sufficient pool from which to locate a sharply struck coin. Note the strong die clash that has partially obscured the U of UNUM in this example.

As befits its high mintage, there are more than the usual number of off-center strikes and other errors (see Chapter 3). Another flaw associated with this issue is poor mixing of the alloy. This resulted in coins having coppery streaks on their surfaces from concentrations of copper that did not blend evenly with the nickel metal. These may have been just small spots in the ingot, but when rolled out into long ribbons of metal for the blanking press these spots are drawn into the long streaks that produce such "woodgrain" toning. Due to this and other production problems, the luster on 1920-P nickels ranges from mediocre all the way to excellent.

While California and other western states had largely overcome their old prejudices against cents and nickels early in the century, such was not the case in remote Alaska. The August 1920 issue of *The Numismatist* reported, "Though luxury taxes in Alaska call for small coins, the Yukon Development League has rejected a proposal to introduce dimes and nickels into local circulation. Dawson never has had any smaller coin than the 25-cent piece, and will adhere to it."

1920-D

Mintage:
9,418,000
(Ranking 33/64)

Popular Varieties:

A boldly repunched mintmark variety exists (RPM-1, FS-016.63).

At least two cud breaks are known for this issue, one giving the bison his familiar hat and the other taking away part of the word CENTS.

RPM-1
(Tom Miller)

Rarity:

The 1920-D nickel is a very scarce coin in the higher circulated grades and in all mint state grades. It is particularly elusive in the most popular grades of VF-AU.

RATINGS: G-VG R2, **F** R3, **VF** R4, **XF-AU** R4, **MS60-63** R4, **MS64** R4, **MS65** R5

TOTAL MS PCGS/NGC = 435 (Ranking 8/64)

Values:

	1940	1950	1960	1970	1980	1990	2000
G	——	.55	1.25	2.50	3.00	3.00	5.50
F	——	1.75	5.00	9.00	8.75	8.75	17.00
XF	——	——	35.00	55.00	55.00	100.00	220.00
MS60	3.00	32.50	80.00	195.00	275.00	——	——
MS63	——	——	——	——	——	700.00	1,100

Comments: Overall rarity is a factor in making this coin difficult to acquire, but striking problems play a greater role. Although not as mushy as 1919-D, it still exhibits a general softness which is most pronounced at the bison's right hind leg and tail.

1920-D nickels typically have disappointing luster. Most are frosty or have the soft, metallic look that has sometimes been described as "liquid mercury." Moderate to deep toning is not unusual for this date, though many have been "dipped" in a mild acid solution to remove their toning. The results of such treatment will vary from somewhat satisfying to complete failure, since deep toning has already impaired the coin's luster. Removing the toning may only make that fact more obvious.

The specimen illustrated exhibits several small die cracks and clash marks at UNUM. Such flaws are very typical of Denver Mint coins of any denomination from the mid-1910s through the early 1920s.

This was the last coinage of nickels at the Denver Mint until 1924. Conventional wisdom, aided by the poorly-researched articles of well-meaning numismatic writers, has long ascribed this drop in production to the fact that the mints were too busy coining silver dollars mandated by the 1918 Pittman Act. In reality, the huge mintages of minor coins prompted by the wartime boom of 1916-20 collided with the severe economic recession of 1921-22. The U. S. Mint director's annual reports clearly reveal that there was simply a glut of coins during the early 1920s, and it wasn't until the latter months of 1923 that a demand appeared for additional pieces.

1920-S

Mintage:
9,689,000
(Ranking 34/64)

Popular Varieties:

One or more varieties are known with a two-feathers obverse (FS-016.631).

At least one obverse cud and two varieties for the reverse are known.

Three-and-a-half legged
(Talbert)

Rarity:

1920-S is another key coin, though it's not as scarce as 1920-D. Low grade pieces seem to have been widely hoarded by collectors and are readily available. While examples in the higher circulated grades may be found at many coin shows, these are almost always quite weakly struck on the reverse. Adequate strikes do turn up, however, and are worth one's patience. In mint state, 1920-S is among the scarcest coins in the series. Gems are very rare.

RATINGS: G-VG R1, **F** R2, **VF** R3, **XF-AU** R3, **MS60-63** R4, **MS64** R5, **MS65** R7

TOTAL MS PCGS/NGC = 495 (Ranking 10/64)

Values:

	1940	1950	1960	1970	1980	1990	2000
G	——	.55	1.25	2.00	1.75	1.75	2.50
F	——	1.75	5.00	8.00	6.25	6.25	13.00
XF	——	——	35.00	48.50	51.50	75.00	150.00
MS60	3.00	35.00	80.00	195.00	285.00	——	——
MS63	——	——	——	——	——	500.00	1,000

Comments:

Well struck coins are scarce and highly prized. Fully struck examples are virtually unknown. Most seen range in strike from fair all the way to awful, the reverse being particularly subject to extreme die erosion and incompleteness. The worst ones look like wax coins left to melt in the sun. The San Francisco Mint may have utilized elderly reverse dies left over from previous years, a seemingly common practice from about 1917 through 1926.

The typical 1920-S nickel has luster that is just so-so. Some are frosty, while others have the metallic sheen described previously as looking like "liquid mercury."

Minor planchet flaws, such as small laminations and streaking, are not uncommon, though they're less of a problem for this date than for 1921-S.

1920-S nickels were widely hoarded in low grades during the 1940s and 1950s, when such coins were still to be found in circulation. As the market for worn pieces declined in later years, their price appreciation was poor until rebounding during the 1990s. In contrast, higher grade nickels have been good performers and will probably continue to be so.

1921

Mintage:
10,663,000
(Ranking 37/64)

Popular Varieties:

A two-feathers variety has the innermost feather partially effaced through vigorous polishing of the obverse die (FS-016.633).

A minor obverse doubled-die variety is also known, this being noticeable in the Indian's eyebrow and nostrils.

Two feathers. FS-016.633
(Fivaz/Stanton)

Rarity:

As a result of its lower than normal mintage, this date is scarcer than most P-Mints in all grades. The 1921-P nickels seem to have been made with greater care, however, and top-notch gems are not hard to find.

RATINGS: G-VG R1, **F** R2, **VF** R3, **XF-AU** R3,
MS60-63 R3, **MS64** R4, **MS65** R4

TOTAL MS PCGS/NGC = 817 (Ranking 26/64)

Values:

	1940	1950	1960	1970	1980	1990	2000
G	——	.15	.35	.75	.85	.85	1.25
F	——	.50	1.25	2.60	3.00	3.00	3.00
XF	——	——	3.00	11.50	14.50	17.00	20.00
MS60	1.25	5.50	11.00	59.00	75.00	——	——
MS63	——	——	——	——	——	190.00	135.00

Comments:

As noted above, 1921-P nickels are typically of higher quality than most entries in this series. Both strike and luster are almost universally excellent. Satiny pieces may be found, but the majority display very bright and frosty luster.

The only negative with this date is a slightly higher than usual incidence of laminated planchets, perhaps reflecting a change in the Philadelphia Mint's supplier. During and after World War I, the U. S. Mint alternated between buying planchets ready-made from commercial vendors and producing them in-house. Some statistics were kept on the relative quality of each, but the results were inconclusive. After the mid-1920s, the Mint reverted to producing its own planchets, though in recent years it has relied almost entirely on vendors.

The date 1921 is more boldly engraved in the master die than on previous issues, and this is the only date in the series in which the numeral 1 has a serif. Perhaps this was another attempt at improving the durability of the date. Whatever the reason for this change, numerals of more conventional style were again used when coinage resumed in 1923.

1921-S

Mintage:
1,557,000
(Ranking 6/64)

Popular Varieties:

This is another date for which two-feathers coins are known (FS-016.635)

A retained cud break may be found that obliterates a portion of the date.

Rarity:

1921-S is one of the scarcest Buffaloes in all grades, and its rarity in problem-free condition is compounded by the flaws described below. Difficult to locate in grade VF, it becomes a genuine challenge to find XF-AU coins. Mint state examples of mediocre quality are more available than ones in the higher circulated grades, but they're often afflicted with the same problems.

RATINGS: G-VG R2, **F** R3, **VF** R4, **XF-AU** R5, **MS60-63** R4, **MS64** R4, **MS65** R5

TOTAL MS PCGS/NGC = 325 (Ranking 3/64)

Values:

	1940	1950	1960	1970	1980	1990	2000
G	——	1.00	4.50	9.00	9.25	13.00	22.00
F	——	3.50	9.50	25.00	30.00	40.00	70.00
XF	——	——	40.00	95.00	115.00	325.00	675.00
MS60	3.50	40.00	90.00	335.00	475.00	——	——
MS63	——	——	——	——	——	1,000	1,900

Comments:

This date is particularly subject to laminations and toning streaks, the result of poorly prepared planchet stock. Other signs of hurried work include multiple die cracks and metal flowlines, both evidence of extended die use. The end result is a very challenging coin to find in desirable condition.

In contrast to its other attributes, the 1921-S nickel typically has very good to excellent luster. This is often very bright and frosty due to the eroded state of the dies.

1921-S is another date that is difficult to grade, due to weak strikes and worn dies. Although better struck than most S-Mint nickels of the 1920s, many coins of this date offered as VF-AU may be lacking a complete horn. Grading thus becomes a judgment call based on the amount of overall wear and remaining luster. As always, the high values listed for VF and better coins are for nickels having a fully visible horn.

Attempts to hoard circulated examples during the 1940s and later proved largely unsuccessful, as this date was scarce from its inception.

All of this issue's mintage was coined during the latter half of the year.[4] It's doubtful that any of these coins were needed at the time, and they were probably not released until the coining of nickels resumed late in 1923.

1923

Mintage:
35,715,000
(Ranking 54/64)

Popular Varieties:

None are reported.

Rarity: 1923-P is common in all grades short of gem. The latter are available but scarce. Original rolls may still exist.

RATINGS: G-VG R1, **F** R1, **VF** R2, **XF-AU** R2, **MS60-63** R2, **MS64** R3, **MS65** R4

TOTAL MS PCGS/NGC = 1023 (Ranking 32/64)

Values:

	1940	1950	1960	1970	1980	1990	2000
G	——	.15	.20	.40	.45	.45	1.00
F	——	.40	.60	1.10	1.25	1.25	1.50
XF	——	——	1.50	4.85	7.00	7.00	8.00
MS60	1.00	3.25	6.50	21.00	32.50	——	——
MS63	——	——	——	——	——	90.00	75.00

Comments: The quality of strike will vary from good to excellent. While a few weakly struck examples may be found, most coins of this issue are sharp but not quite fully struck. The luster of 1923-P nickels is almost uniformly outstanding.

Until the past twenty years or so, the 1923-P nickel was lumped in with later P-Mint Buffaloes as a common coin in all grades. This date is now recognized as being scarcer than most other Philadelphia coins in the top grades, though it would be inaccurate to describe it as rare.

1923-S

Mintage:
6,142,000
(Ranking 21/64)

Popular Varieties:

An S/D variety was once believed to exist, but this is almost certainly just the result of very worn dies on which the S mintmark was distorted through erosion. This problem became increasingly common from 1919 through 1926.

Rarity:

Despite its relatively low mintage, this date is available in all grades short of gem for the collector who is not too particular about strike. Grading services do not place much emphasis on striking quality, so a high grade is no indicator of a sharp coin. The more discriminating and patient buyer will await the few well struck coins that sometimes appear.

RATINGS: G-VG R1, **F** R2, **VF** R3, **XF-AU** R3, **MS60-63** R3, **MS64** R4, **MS65** R6

TOTAL MS PCGS/NGC = 704 (Ranking 19/64)

Values:

	1940	1950	1960	1970	1980	1990	2000
G	——	.40	1.00	1.50	1.50	1.50	2.50
F	——	1.50	4.50	6.00	5.50	5.50	9.00
XF	——	——	29.00	42.50	50.00	60.00	225.00
MS60	3.50	35.00	65.00	165.00	225.00	——	——
MS63	——	——	——	——	——	400.00	650.00

Comments:

Examples having adequate strikes do turn up, but fully struck pieces are rare. Like 1920-S, this date is often seen with a strong obverse and a mushy reverse, the result of overextended die use. This suggests that reverse dies were retained from previous years. Worn dies may reveal themselves also through a ridge of slightly raised metal running just inside the coin's borders. This is due to a sinking of the dies from continual compression. The hard alloy and broad die cavities of the Buffalo Nickel made this coin type particularly subject to this form of die erosion, though it's commonly seen also on Lincoln Cents and Indian Head Quarter Eagles.

Most 1923-S nickels have good to excellent luster that is either satiny or frosty. The latter are far more common, as the satiny quality of the dies was quickly lost to wear. Toning of varying depth is often seen for this date, though it's rarely an asset. Most typical is monochromatic toning of golden brown, though some examples may have very pretty rainbow toning around the peripheries.

Extensively hoarded in low grades during the 1940s and 1950s, the 1923-S nickel is another issue whose value in grades G-F peaked during the early 1960s at the height of the coin collecting boom. Stalled for decades afterward, only during the 1990s did the resurgent popularity of circulated coins prompt something of a recovery. Still, after adjusting for inflation, the $9.00 F of 2000 is worth far less than the $4.50 coin purchased in 1960. This reflects a major shift in the coin market during that period and is more fully described in Chapter 2.

The production of nickels at the San Francisco Mint had been suspended for nearly two years when it resumed in the latter months in 1923.

1924

Mintage:
21,620,000
(Ranking 46/64)

Popular Varieties:

Some are lacking the designer's initial F, the result of overpolishing the die. This was usually done in response to a die clash that left inverted impressions of each opposing die.

An obverse retained cud is known running along the top of the Indian's head. It's possible that this variety may yet be found with the break complete, as well.

Rarity:

1924-P nickels are much less common than their mintage suggests. Low-grade coins are available, but XF-AU examples can be elusive. In mint state, all grades short of gem may be found, but in smaller quantities than for 1925 and later P-Mints. The certified population of mint state coins is notably low.

RATINGS: G-VG R2, **F** R2, **VF** R2, **XF-AU** R3, **MS60-63** R3, **MS64** R3, **MS65** R4

TOTAL MS PCGS/NGC = 710 (Ranking 21/64)

Values:

	1940	1950	1960	1970	1980	1990	2000
G	——	.15	.20	.40	.45	.45	1.00
F	——	.40	.50	1.20	1.25	1.25	1.50
XF	——	——	1.75	4.80	8.00	8.00	10.00
MS60	1.00	4.00	8.50	22.50	55.00	——	——
MS63	——	——	——	——	——	135.00	85.00

Comments:

1924-P nickels are often seen weakly struck, the hair above the bison's forehead and foreleg being incomplete. Since such weakness is common to all examples seen, it may reflect an incomplete hubbing of the master die. It's hard to imagine such a careless mistake being made for the important master die, but then quality seemed to be a low priority at the U. S. Mint during the 1920s. A slight softness in the first two digits of the date is a precursor of worse things to come in 1925.

1924-P nickels typically have just average to good luster. Coins with strong eye appeal are very rare.

1924-D

Mintage:
5,258,000
(Ranking 15/64)

Popular Varieties:

A very large cud break is known for the reverse that progressively took out much of the die from 2-4 o'clock.

Rarity:

1924-D is scarce and among the least available of the D-Mint nickels, though it is not as rare in mint state as its overall rarity would suggest. Choice and gem examples are a bit more available than for most mintmarked coins of the period.

RATINGS: G-VG R2, **F** R2, **VF** R3, **XF-AU** R4, **MS60-63** R3, **MS64** R3, **MS65** R4

TOTAL MS PCGS/NGC = 559 (Ranking 13/64)

Values:

	1940	1950	1960	1970	1980	1990	2000
G	——	.35	1.00	2.00	2.25	2.25	3.50
F	——	1.50	4.00	8.00	7.75	8.00	12.00
XF	——	——	22.50	48.00	45.00	85.00	150.00
MS60	4.00	30.00	62.50	175.00	285.00	——	——
MS63	——	——	——	——	——	450.00	650.00

Comments:

Coins with fair to good strikes may be found, but fully struck pieces may be unknown. A flat forehead on the bison is typical for this date and probably reflects a deficiency in the master die itself. Examples with more head definition often have weak tails, a common problem associated with incomplete metal displacement.

This issue represents the first coinage of nickels at Denver since 1920. There was simply no need for additional pieces until this time, since so many had been produced during the war years. Even then, the demand for fresh coins during the 1920s remained subject to regional fluctuations. Some of the Denver Mint coins of all denominations languished in Midwest bank vaults for years until finally being released during the economic recovery of the late 1930s. While it's not certain that the 1924-D nickels fell into this category, there are other issues known to have turned up in quantity years after they were made.

Among the coins that subsequently became quite common in mint state after initially being thought of as rare were 1931-S, 1932 and 1932-D cents, 1926-D, 1928-D, 1930-S and 1931-S nickels, 1929-D and 1931-D dimes and 1926-D quarters. All were partially held back from issue at the time of their coining and released in quantity a few years later, by which time speculators were waiting to pounce on them.

1924-S

Mintage:
1,437,000
(Ranking 4/64)

Popular Varieties: A single repunched mintmark variety is reported.

Rarity: Seemingly the most difficult date in the series in grades VF-AU, 1924-S is also quite rare in mint state. Although largely spared the technical problems that plague other key dates, it is rare by virtue of its poor survivorship in desirable grades. 1924-S nickels are much scarcer than the vaunted 1926-S in grades VF-AU, though both are rare in mint state. In fact, these two dates are tied for first/second place with the lowest certified mint state populations.

RATINGS: G-VG R2, **F** R3, **VF** R5, **XF-AU** R5, **MS60-63** R4, **MS64** R4, **MS65** R6

TOTAL MS PCGS/NGC = 257 (Ranking 1-2/64)

Values:

	1940	1950	1960	1970	1980	1990	2000
G	——	.90	2.75	5.25	4.50	4.50	6.00
F	——	3.00	9.50	16.50	14.50	14.50	45.00
XF	——	——	45.00	115.00	140.00	400.00	1,000
MS60	4.00	45.00	110.00	675.00	800.00	——	——
MS63	——	——	——	——	——	1,450	2,900

Comments: Most 1924-S nickels seen are adequately struck in general terms. Fully struck pieces are seldom available, a situation that is aggravated by the relatively small population of mint state coins for this date. The biggest striking deficiency seems to be the bison's horn, which is frequently incomplete.

Caution should be exercised when purchasing one of the many examples that are offered as Very Fine or even Extremely Fine but that lack the full length of the bison's horn. Quite a number of these have been certified and encapsulated in recent years on the basis of overall wear, at best an unsatisfying compromise. The high prices listed for this and other key dates in VF and higher grades are for coins with full-length horns. Determining the value of hornless VF-XF-AU nickels is a guessing game.

In low grades, 1924-S is yet another issue that performed poorly between 1960 and 1990, only to make an impressive recovery during the '90s. All of the key dates were extensively hoarded during the 1940s and '50s in whatever grade they were found. When the coin market included many thousands of unsophisticated hobbyists who simply wanted to fill the holes in their albums, there existed a strong demand for low-grade pieces. The increasing sophistication of coin buyers since that time led to a greater emphasis on quality over completeness throughout the 1970s and '80s. But with the resurgent popularity of the Buffalo Nickel series in recent years, demand for all grades is finally beginning to grow once again.

1925

Mintage:
35,565,100
(Ranking 53/64)

Popular Varieties:

As with all nickels dated 1925 from each of the three mints, this issue exhibits slight doubling along the left side of the left hair ribbon. This feature was evidently inherent in the master die for 1925.

On one variety, part of AMERICA is obliterated by a cud break. This was probably the consequence of a die clashing, as deep clash marks are visible within the Latin legend.

Rarity:

1925-P is common in all grades short of gem. These too are available but do not possess a fully struck date. Original rolls may still exist.

RATINGS: **G-VG** R1, **F** R1, **VF** R2, **XF-AU** R2, **MS60-63** R2, **MS64** R2, **MS65** R4

TOTAL MS PCGS/NGC = 1076 (Ranking 35/64)

Values:

	1940	1950	1960	1970	1980	1990	2000
G	——	.10	.15	.40	.50	.45	1.50
F	——	.30	.50	1.15	1.25	1.25	2.50
XF	——	——	1.50	4.75	7.00	7.00	8.00
MS60	1.00	3.00	8.50	22.50	30.00	——	——
MS63	——	——	——	——	——	90.00	70.00

Comments:

The 1925-P nickel is an odd coin. It is never badly struck, but nor is it ever quite fully struck. All examples seem to have a slightly incomplete look that probably resulted from deficiencies in the master dies. This is true of several P-Mint dates starting with 1919 and lasting through most of the 1920s.

On the plus side, this issue usually features excellent luster. A bit more subdued than for some other dates, it is nonetheless pleasing. All pieces seen have frosty luster, satiny pieces being unknown to me.

1925-D

Mintage:
4,450,000
(Ranking 13/64)

Popular Varieties:

All possess the slight obverse doubling common to 1925-dated nickels from all three mints.

A two-feathers variety exists for this date (FS-016.638)

D or S?
(Talbert)

Rarity:

In problem-free, well struck condition this is one of the most difficult dates in the series. Poor strikes are so extreme that even low grade coins are affected, these being difficult to grade and value. In grades VF-AU it is a very challenging coin to locate. Mediocre mint state coins are not rare, but truly choice and gem pieces are very elusive.

RATINGS: **G-VG** R2, **F** R3, **VF** R4, **XF-AU** R5, **MS60-63** R4, **MS64** R4, **MS65** R5

TOTAL MS PCGS/NGC = 659 (Ranking 16/64)

Values:

	1940	1950	1960	1970	1980	1990	2000
G	——	.50	2.50	4.00	3.50	3.50	5.25
F	——	1.75	7.50	12.00	11.00	11.00	25.00
XF	——	——	17.50	50.00	65.00	90.00	150.00
MS60	2.50	15.00	33.00	210.00	300.00	——	——
MS63	——	——	——	——	——	550.00	575.00

Comments:

Well struck examples may be found but are rare in all grades. The worst strikes rival 1919-D, 1919-S, 1920-S, 1925-S and 1926-D for flatness in the bison's head. Even mint state coins may show little or no sign of the bison's horn, while very few have complete horns. Some 1925-D nickels are known with the E in FIVE filled, and all are characteristically weak in the first two numerals of the date.

This is another coin whose values in the lower grades languished throughout the 1970s and '80s, when only mint state coins received any attention from the marketplace. Since the first edition of this book was published in 1992, all circulated grades for 1925-D have enjoyed a satisfying recovery. It seems that a new generation of collectors has rediscovered these coins.

1925-S

Mintage:
6,256,000
(Ranking 22/64)

Popular Varieties:

Slight doubling in the Indian's hair ribbon is normal for all coins of this date.

Perhaps the most desirable variety is the prominent repunched mintmark (RPM-1, FS-016.64).

A two-feathers obverse may also be found (FS-016.641).

At least one variety is missing the designer's initial F, probably the consequence of a filled or overly polished die.

Finally, one obverse features a retained cud affecting the date area.

RPM-1a
(Tom Miller)

Rarity:

Although readily available in lower grades, this date is scarce in grades VF-AU, due in no small part to striking deficiencies. Low-end mint state coins are scarce, while fully struck choice and gem pieces are genuinely rare.

RATINGS: **G-VG** R1, **F** R2, **VF** R3, **XF-AU** R4, **MS60-63** R4, **MS64** R6, **MS65** R7

TOTAL MS PCGS/NGC = 564 (Ranking 12/64)

Values:

	1940	1950	1960	1970	1980	1990	2000
G	——	.60	2.50	2.50	2.25	2.25	3.00
F	——	2.50	7.50	8.50	6.75	6.75	12.00
XF	——	——	30.00	48.00	52.50	55.00	140.00
MS60	5.00	50.00	100.00	230.00	300.00	——	——
MS63	——	——	——	——	——	450.00	1,700

Comments:

Overall weakness is the norm for this issue, particularly in the bison's head and around the coin's periphery. It seems that both broad set distances between the dies and overextended usage of the dies combined to produce so many miserable coins. In extreme cases, the reverse die is so worn that its mintmark is grossly distorted and even indecipherable. Such coins are returned by grading services without a decision. More common are examples having incomplete dates, the first two numerals being washed out. Along with 1919-D, 1919-S, 1920-S, 1925-D and 1926-S, this is one of the most poorly struck dates in the series.

1925-S nickels typically have just average to good luster. In combination with their generally mushy appearance, the aesthetic value of this issue is low, regardless of its certified grade. Collectors, whatever their budget, buy this date simply to complete their sets.

The 1925-S nickel was another long-term loser in the lower grades for many years, only to enjoy a promising recovery during the 1990s. Such coins were extensively hoarded from the time that collecting from circulation first became popular, during the mid-1930s, until the better date Buffaloes disappeared entirely from circulation, around 1960.

1926

Mintage:
44,693,000
(Ranking 57/64)

Popular Varieties: None are reported.

Rarity: This is the most common date in all grades since 1913 Type 1. Original rolls are likely to exist, while gem singles are always available for a price.

RATINGS: **G-VG** R1, **F** R1, **VF** R2, **XF-AU** R2, **MS60-63** R2, **MS64** R2, **MS65** R2

TOTAL MS PCGS/NGC = 2127 (Ranking 55/64)

Values:

	1940	1950	1960	1970	1980	1990	2000
G	——	.15	.15	.35	.40	.40	.75
F	——	.25	.35	.95	.95	.95	1.00
XF	——	——	1.00	4.75	5.00	5.00	5.00
MS60	1.25	2.25	6.00	18.00	27.00	——	——
MS63	——	——	——	——	——	80.00	50.00

Comments: Most seen are well struck, though the dies were sometimes used until they became worn and heavily flowlined. Areas of roughness typically formed on the Indian's neck and below his chin as the result of this extensive metal flow. There may be some incompleteness of strike in the Indian's braid knot and in the highest points of the bison's hide, but enough mint state pieces survive that one can be choosy.

1926-P nickels are almost always highly lustrous. Their luster is typically quite frosty, but the depth of the frost will vary according to how worn the dies were.

The popularity of the Buffalo Nickel was international during the 1920s, as this account from *The Numismatist* reveals:

Dr. Gustave Alexander, professor of the University of Vienna, is attending a joint session of the Interstate Post-Graduate Association and the Kansas City Southwest Clinical Society, in session at Kansas City. In an interview with him the Kansas City Star says:

"He says prettier things about Kansas City, and all America, too, for that matter, than almost any visitor we have had from foreign shores for a long time. He likes America's coinage, for instance. He keeps a ready supply of buffalo nickels in his pocket because he believes they are so beautiful. What? You never saw any beauty in a buffalo nickel yourself? Neither did the writer, but he got a fine calling down from Dr. Alexander for that lack of appreciation.

" 'I believe sincerely the American 5-cent piece is the most beautiful coin in the world,' Dr. Alexander says. 'The head of the Indian is perfect and the head of the buffalo is, too. The dimensions are as good as they were on the old Greek coins, which were supposed to have been classics for all time.' "[5]

1926-D

Mintage:
5,638,000
(Ranking 19/64)

Popular Varieties:

Some examples are known with their reverses rotated from the normal 180-degree alignment with the obverse. Technically, it is the obverse die that was out of alignment, being in the lower or anvil position. Had the reverse die, which was in the upper or hammer position for Buffalo Nickels, been loose, it may conceivably have fallen from the press. Rotated dies are actually mint errors rather varieties, since there is nothing wrong with the actual dies. This phenomenon occurs with a few other dates in the Buffalo series, but there doesn't seem to be much premium attached to this form of error.

Rarity:

Although not particularly scarce in most grades, the majority are so poorly struck as to render them undesirable to collectors. Gems are scarce for the same reason, though not as difficult to find as for 1925-D.

RATINGS: G-VG R2, **F** R2, **VF** R3, **XF-AU** R3, **MS60-63** R2, **MS64** R4, **MS65** R4

TOTAL MS PCGS/NGC = 806 (Ranking 23/64)

Values:

	1940	1950	1960	1970	1980	1990	2000
G	——	.15	.50	2.40	2.00	2.00	3.50
F	——	.50	1.00	10.00	9.00	9.00	16.00
XF	——	——	2.25	50.00	60.00	90.00	110.00
MS60	.50	4.50	10.00	315.00	300.00	——	——
MS63	——	——	——	——	——	425.00	450.00

Comments:

This date has long been cited as the most difficult to find fully struck, probably due to a citation in R. S. Yeoman's *A Guide Book of United States Coins*. While most 1926-D nickels are indeed found with extremely worn dies, particularly on the reverse, the problem is no worse than for 1919-D, 1919-S, 1920-S, 1925-D and 1925-S.

The number of PCGS/NGC certified coins would likely be higher were it not for the fact that the poor quality of most uncirculated 1926-D nickels discourages submissions. Many mint state coins lack a three-dimensional horn, this being either quite flat or lacking altogether.

The luster for this date is average or below average for the series. Most are frosty, but with subdued brilliance.

1926-D nickels were among the few dates in this series withheld from immediate release, at least to some extent. Considered a rarity until the late 1930s, rolls suddenly became available when increasing prosperity drew down the supply of available coins to the bottom of the vaults.

This issue was among the key and semi-key coins widely hoarded by collectors while they were still obtainable in circulation. This contributed to depressing the value of worn examples throughout the 1970s and '80s. Only with the resurgent popularity of circulated coins during the 1990s did values once again advance.

1926-S

Mintage:
970,000
(Ranking 1/64)

Popular Varieties: None are reported.

Rarity: Long hailed as the rarest date in the series because it has the lowest mintage of any regular issue, the 1926-S seems overrated in the popular grades of VF-XF. Only in AU and above does this coin's reputation hold true. Mint state examples are very scarce, gems nearly unknown. This date is tied with 1924-S as having the lowest certified mint state populations.

RATINGS: G-VG R2, **F** R3, **VF** R3, **XF-AU** R4, **MS60-63** R5, **MS64** R5, **MS65** R7

TOTAL MS PCGS/NGC = 257 (Ranking 1-2/64)

Values:

	1940	1950	1960	1970	1980	1990	2000
G	——	.60	1.65	4.75	5.50	5.50	8.00
F	——	3.00	12.50	16.50	15.50	14.00	35.00
XF	——	——	60.00	115.00	150.00	300.00	750.00
MS60	10.00	70.00	165.00	440.00	625.00	——	——
MS63	——	——	——	——	——	1,300	5,000

Comments: Worn reverse dies are the norm for 1926-S. These were probably leftovers from previous years, since dateless dies could be used until they failed completely. Weakness in the bison's head is common enough that many examples offered as VF and XF do not meet the criteria for these grades and have been assigned them simply on the basis of overall wear. Well struck coins are worth a substantial premium over lesser examples.

1926-S nickels have good luster and were struck on well made planchets. They are sometimes found with unattractive toning of golden brown, and this problem likewise affects pieces in the higher circulated grades.

Due to its low mintage and genuine scarcity, the hoarders who squirreled away every key date Buffalo Nickel they could find in circulation enjoyed only limited success in locating this issue.

In the first edition of this book, published in 1992, I made the observation that 1926-S nickels grading F seemed undervalued. The market evidently agreed, as revealed by the price advance from 1990 to 2000. Similarly impressive gains were registered in all grades for this rare and highly sought coin.

1927

Mintage:
37,981,000
(Ranking 56/64)

Popular Varieties:

A doubled-die obverse is reported by Leroy and Marilyn Van Allen.

Rarity:

This issue is common in all grades, though slightly less so than 1926-P. Original rolls likely exist, but these are quickly broken up when they enter the market from old collections.

RATINGS: G-VG R1, **F** R1, **VF** R2, **XF-AU** R2, **MS60-63** R2, **MS64** R2, **MS65** R3

TOTAL MS PCGS/NGC = 1434 (Ranking 43/64)

Values:

	1940	1950	1960	1970	1980	1990	2000
G	——	.10	.15	.35	.40	.40	.75
F	——	.25	.45	.85	.95	.95	1.00
XF	——	——	1.00	4.00	5.00	5.00	5.00
MS60	1.00	2.50	5.00	15.50	26.00	——	——
MS63	——	——	——	——	——	75.00	45.00

Comments:

Well struck coins are the norm for this issue, though no Buffalo Nickel coined 1918 or later will have the sharpness of well struck coins from earlier years. The master hubs for this type gradually became worn, a process accelerated by the high mintages of 1916-20.

1927-P nickels typically have very good to excellent luster. Satiny pieces are occasionally seen, but the vast majority display the frosty brilliance that characterizes most issues from the 1920s and '30s.

Five coins described as specimen strikes or satin finish proofs have surfaced since 1989. See Chapter 7 for more information.

In his book, *Making Money,* Edward Rochette revealed how the mintage of 1927 nickels was supplemented through the private and quite illegal operation run by three individuals in Monroe, New York. In March of 1935, state troopers searching in the woods for a still stumbled upon an abandoned farmhouse. Found within its cellar was a "machine shop, stamping press, boxes of blank planchets, 3,400 finished 1927 Buffalo nickels and a sizeable quantity of raw metal."

The troopers uncovered an illegal mint that had been flooding a five-state region with fake nickels for a year or more. Allegedly, some five million five-cent pieces of this date were counterfeited by brothers Louis and George Ehlers and their partner, Leo Gailie. The trio had assembled a network of fences who purchased the coins at a rate of fifty cents on the dollar, netting the manufacturers a profit of just two cents per coin.

1927-D

Mintage:
5,730,000
(Ranking 20/64)

Popular Varieties:

The most interesting variety for this date has a triple-punched mintmark (RPM-1, FS-016.7)

Aggressive polishing of the reverse die produced the 3-1/2 leg variety (FS-016.65)

A two-feathers variety is also reported.

Minor die doubling is known for the reverse.

Cuds include one giving the bison a small cap and another affecting OF AMERICA.

D/D/D RPM-1
(Tom Miller)

Rarity:

This is a date that seems underrated in grades XF and AU. I said so in the 1992 edition of this book, and I still believe it to be true. In gem mint state the same may be said, with well struck examples being particularly elusive.

RATINGS: **G-VG** R2, **F** R2, **VF** R3, **XF-AU** R4, **MS60-63** R2, **MS64** R3, **MS65** R5

TOTAL MS PCGS/NGC = 809 (Ranking 24-25/64)

Values:

	1940	1950	1960	1970	1980	1990	2000
G	——	.15	.60	1.00	1.00	1.00	1.25
F	——	.50	1.50	3.75	3.00	3.00	4.00
XF	——	——	3.50	15.00	20.00	35.00	40.00
MS60	2.00	5.50	14.00	45.00	65.00	——	——
MS63	——	——	——	——	——	250.00	235.00

Comments:

Fully struck coins are rare, though examples having a reasonably good strike are more available than for 1925-D and 1926-D.

1927-D nickels typically have just average to good luster. Heavily worn dies produced a rich, frosty quality, and this may appeal to some collectors.

Though World War I had brought about 50% inflation in the value of the dollar, the purchasing power of the humble nickel remained significant at this time, as suggested by the following account from 1927:

In the first place, the purchasing range of the nickel is so wide that it includes every one in America. There is no class excluded, even the so-called "panhandlers," for that is the denomination customarily mentioned in their sidewalk solicitations.

For five cents one can buy everything from a cup of coffee to a stone-set ring–from a sandwich to a reprint of Omar Khayyam. A check-up of articles sold for a nickel in one five-and-ten-cent store revealed some 800 different items, including radio parts, toilet goods, soap, rubber sundries, hardware, kitchen utensils, stationery, phonograph supplies and candy.

One cannot travel many miles in the United States without in some way utilizing the five-cent piece. Several great industries have been built around it and use it as the main purchasing unit–the automat cafeterias and armchair lunch rooms, trolley transportation systems, chewing gum and chocolate packet makers, and even some of the greatest of our periodicals. The public telephone probably owes its success as a national institution to the fact that it functions on the nickel-in-the-slot basis. The tremendous sale of newspapers upon the city streets calls for an increasingly large amount of small change, in which the nickel plays a leading part.[6]

1927-S

Mintage:
3,430,000
(Ranking 8/64)

Popular Varieties:

Walter Breen reported a doubled-die obverse (B-2630), and Bill Fivaz confirms its existence.

Rarity:

Scarce in mint state, 1927-S is genuinely rare in choice and gem condition. Low grade circulated pieces are abundant, but problem-free examples are very scarce in grades VF-AU.

RATINGS: **G-VG** R1, **F** R2, **VF** R3, **XF-AU** R3, **MS60-63** R4, **MS64** R4, **MS65** R6

TOTAL MS PCGS/NGC = 453 (Ranking 9/64)

Values:

	1940	1950	1960	1970	1980	1990	2000
G	——	.60	1.35	1.30	1.00	1.00	1.00
F	——	3.00	8.50	6.50	3.00	3.00	2.25
XF	——	——	40.00	45.00	41.00	60.00	65.00
MS60	15.00	70.00	130.00	250.00	300.00	——	——
MS63	——	——	——	——	——	325.00	1,800

Comments:

1927-S is generally well struck for an S-Mint nickel of the 1920s, and uncirculated pieces may exhibit highly polished, prooflike surfaces.

VF and XF coins do turn up with some regularity, but they are often found with problems such as scratches and harsh cleaning. AU examples seem to be fairly scarce, although problem coins are less often encountered in this grade.

This date enjoyed a very larger price advance in MS63 condition between 1990 and 2000. The same cannot be said for circulated pieces. While I consider the XF valuation to be a bit low for problem-free examples, there do seem to be more low-grade 1927-S nickels than the market can absorb. This date was widely hoarded by earlier generations of collectors, and its track record has been abysmal. When the popularity of collecting coins from circulation peaked in the early 1960s, there were enough collectors to sustain a demand than simply doesn't exist anymore. While most of the key and semi-key Buffaloes have rebounded during the past ten years, the 1927-S nickel has continued to languish.

During World War II, 1927-S nickels were still fairly plentiful, as revealed by this letter from "A Soldier in Hawaii" published in *The Numismatist*:

Those scarce 1942 P nickels are plentiful here so I'll gather a few million of them and bring them back. The only fun I get here is buying a few rolls of nickels, dimes or quarters and looking them over to see what the general run is. Not much luck but there are quite a few 27-S nickels around. This being a numismatist without anyone to talk to or trade with is pretty tough.[7]

1928

Mintage:
23,411,000
(Ranking 48/64)

Popular Varieties:

A 2-1/2-leg variety was reported in the October 1943 issue of *Numismatic Scrapbook Magazine,* but this was doubtless one of the many crude counterfeits circulating during the 1930s and '40s.

Rarity:

1928-P nickels are common in all grades, though they appear to be slightly scarcer than 1927-P and 1929-P. Original rolls may exist, but these will be broken up and sent to the grading services whenever old collections resurface.

RATINGS: G-VG R1, **F** R1, **VF** R2, **XF-AU** R2, **MS60-63** R2, **MS64** R2, **MS65** R3

TOTAL MS PCGS/NGC = 1155 (Ranking 37/64)

Values:

	1940	1950	1960	1970	1980	1990	2000
G	——	——	.10	.35	.40	.40	.75
F	——	.20	.25	.80	.95	.95	1.00
XF	——	——	.75	3.75	4.50	4.50	5.00
MS60	.75	2.00	4.50	16.00	26.00	——	——
MS63	——	——	——	——	——	75.00	50.00

Comments:

The strike for this issue is usually good, but not quite as sharp as for other P-Mints of the late 1920s. In addition, the placement of the date may give the illusion that the 8 is not distinctly separated from the hair ribbon.

1928-P typically possess very bright and pleasing luster. Frosty examples are the norm, and these don't seem to have been coined from heavily worn dies to the extent that other issues were. This quality is partially offset, however, by the slight weakness of strike described above.

The Annual Report of the Director of the Mint for Fiscal Year 1928 reveals that a chromium plating plant was installed at the Philadelphia Mint "for greatly improving the wearing qualities of dies, coin collars, machinery parts, and models." This may explain, at least in part, why the coins from this point onward are less often seen with evidence of having been struck from extremely worn dies.

Further noted by the director was that "Mechanical handling has also been applied to nickel coinage metal, which is purchased in the form of shot." Not all of the nickel arrived in shot form, however, as another section of the report indicated that "there were purchased at the mint at Philadelphia 13,898,011.45 troy ounces of minor-coinage metals at a cost of $228,439.03, which includes 4,451,657.29 troy ounces in nickel blanks prepared for stamping, costing $138,963.45."

1928-D

Mintage:
6,436,000
(Ranking 23/64)

Popular Varieties:

A doubled obverse die is reported, but this variety doesn't seem to have impressed collectors. It may turn out to be merely an example of strike doubling, a common phenomenon with Buffalo Nickels, particularly on their obverses.

Rarity:

This date is very common in mint state. Although gems are elusive, choice pieces are always available. VF-AU coins are less often seen, but their value is held in check by the abundance of uncirculated nickels. The latter may still exist in roll quantities, due to the unique nature of their distribution as described below.

RATINGS: **G-VG** R1, **F** R2, **VF** R3, **XF-AU** R4, **MS60-63** R2, **MS64** R2, **MS65** R4

TOTAL MS PCGS/NGC = 1921 (Ranking 51/64)

Values:

	1940	1950	1960	1970	1980	1990	2000
G	——	——	.15	.40	.75	.75	.90
F	——	.25	.45	1.40	2.25	2.25	2.25
XF	——	——	1.25	4.75	8.00	11.00	15.00
MS60	.50	1.50	4.50	17.50	30.00	——	——
MS63	——	——	——	——	——	110.00	75.00

Comments:

The strike on most 1928-D nickels is typically mediocre, and full strikes form a minority of the many mint state coins available.

Whatever deficiencies this issue displays in strike are partially offset by their superior luster. Most 1928-D nickels are quite bright and pleasing.

This seems to be among the first dates affected by the nationwide economic slowdown of the late 1920s, a condition that ultimately led to the Great Depression. It's known that dates such as 1930-S and 1931-S were held back from release until 1934-35, as no demand existed for additional nickel coinage at the time of their striking. The fact that so many mint state specimens of a fairly low mintage date are available suggests that 1928-D nickels were not released in quantity during that year. Indeed, this date was considered scarce until the late 1930s, at which time it seemed that nearly every dealer in the Midwest had one or more rolls for sale. The recovering economy probably drew down the existing stocks of coins until the bottom of the vaults were reached, at which time this and other issues from previous years were finally freed. Within a few years these hoards were mostly dispersed, but 1928-D nickels are still occasionally seen in quantity even today.

1928-S

Mintage:
6,936,000
(Ranking 24/64)

Popular Varieties:

None are reported, though a large S variety may await discovery (see Comments).

Rarity:

This is another date that is readily available in lower grades, due to the usual hoarding of S-Mint nickels. XF-AU examples are scarce and may also be disappointing in strike. So-so mint state coins are not rare but are much less available than the 1928-D nickels. Choice specimens are scarce, gems rare, due primarily to deficiencies in strike.

RATINGS: **G-VG** R1, **F** R1, **VF** R2, **XF-AU** R3, **MS60-63** R3, **MS64** R3, **MS65** R5

TOTAL MS PCGS/NGC = 690 (Ranking 18/64)

Values:

	1940	1950	1960	1970	1980	1990	2000
G	——	——	.25	.60	.75	.75	.85
F	——	.40	.85	2.00	1.50	1.50	2.00
XF	——	——	3.00	8.75	9.50	10.00	13.00
MS60	1.00	7.50	24.00	52.50	75.00	——	——
MS63	——	——	——	——	——	175.00	550.00

Comments:

Although not as poorly struck as the worst S-Mint nickels, full strikes are rare. Most examples display a general softness in the date, the mintmark and the bison's forehead. The specimen shown above is exceptional.

1928-S nickels have good to excellent luster, though it is rarely of the frostiness associated with most other issues, particularly the P-Mint coins. More commonly seen for this date is the bright, liquid appearance associated with polished planchets that have not been fully compressed by the dies. In addition, some 1928-S nickels are slightly darker than normal in color, due to some peculiar quality of the planchet stock employed.

Every coin seen has been of the usual small S variety. Since all of the other denominations minted at San Francisco in 1928 excepting the dollar are already known with both small and large S mintmarks, this anomaly may exist for the nickel as well. Circumstantial evidence reveals that the large S punch was not used until late in that year, and this suggests that the mintage of 1928-S nickels was probably produced before its employment.

1929

Mintage:
36,446,000
(Ranking 55/64)

Popular Varieties:

There is a good doubled-die obverse, the doubling being most visible in and around date (DDO-2, FS-016.8).

DDO-2
(Fivaz/Stanton)

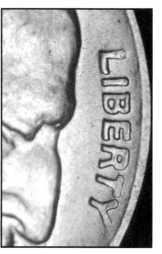

DDO-2
(Fivaz/Stanton)

Rarity: 1929-P is very common in all grades except fully struck gem, but even the latter are available for a price. Original rolls may still exist.

RATINGS: **G-VG** R1, **F** R1, **VF** R2, **XF-AU** R2, **MS60-63** R2, **MS64** R2, **MS65** R3

TOTAL MS PCGS/NGC = 1423 (Ranking 42/64)

Values:

	1940	1950	1960	1970	1980	1990	2000
G	——	——	——	.35	.40	.40	.75
F	——	.15	.15	.75	.85	.85	1.00
XF	——	——	.75	2.50	4.00	4.00	4.50
MS60	.15	.75	3.25	11.75	24.00	——	——
MS63	——	——	——	——	——	65.00	45.00

Comments: 1929-P nickels are usually well struck but not fully struck. This is typical of nickels from the 1920s. Partly to blame was wear on the master hubs, but incompletely hubbed dies and greater than optimal die-set distance seems to have contributed to this problem, as well.

The typical 1929-P nickel is sufficiently lustrous, with the soft frostiness so common to nickels from this period. Really blazing examples are rare, as are satiny pieces.

Though it had no program for selling coins directly to collectors in packaged sets, the Treasury Department was aware that hobbyists sought uncirculated examples of the current issues. Circulars issued during 1932 reveal how fresh coins were obtained by the collecting public, and 1929-P nickels were among the pieces that remained available at that time. The complete text of this notice follows:

> These applications must state definitely the coins desired, the mint by which manufactured, the amount and denomination, as well as the purpose for which desired, and they must be accompanied by a remittance in cash or money order payable to the Treasurer of the United States for the full face value of the coins, plus an amount sufficient to cover the postage thereon by first-class mail and the registration fee, if it is decided the shipment must be registered.
>
> In case coins are desired from all three mints it is necessary to include postage, etc., for three different shipments.
>
> Please read these directions carefully and in making your application to the Treasurer see that each foregoing requirement is complied with.[8]

The federal government was evidently not the only source of 1929 nickels around that time, as this account from the *The Numismatist* suggests:

> Counterfeit buffalo nickels of such deceptive workmanship that they might readily pass the inspection of many an experienced coin collector have recently been found in circulation. They are made of an alloy that very closely resembles that of the genuine issues in density and hardness. Two different dies have been noticed, as follows:
>
> 1928 – A small, rather indistinct pellet in the obverse field just above the Indian's forehead, caused apparently by a slight dent or depression in the die. A very minute die crack in confluence with the lower part of the right hair cord. Another slight diagonal crack in that portion of the exergue field following the word "CENTS."
>
> 1929 – A sharp break in the obverse die, connecting the smaller feather-tip with the edge. A very sleight "pellet" in the field, between the "Y" of "Liberty" and the tip of the Indian's nose.
>
> Both of the above counterfeits have several peculiarities in common. The surface of the pieces has, on the whole, a slightly "uneven" or cloudy appearance, particularly noticeable in the field. In both examples the hair cord partly covers the last figure of the date. However, the most dependable defect to look for is found in the signature, just below the date. In the counterfeits the incuse letter, "F," is either completely illegible or entirely lacking.[9]

1929-D

Mintage:
8,370,000
(Ranking 32/64)

Popular Varieties:

None are reported.

Rarity: As is true of most issues after 1926, this date is common in lower grades. It seems, however, to be unusually scarce in grades XF-AU. Choice mint state coins seem to be available, but gems are elusive, due primarily to deficiencies in strike. Original rolls may exist.

RATINGS: G-VG R1, **F** R2, **VF** R2, **XF-AU** R3, **MS60-63** R3, **MS64** R3, **MS65** R4

TOTAL MS PCGS/NGC = 924 (Ranking 29/64)

Values:

	1940	1950	1960	1970	1980	1990	2000
G	——	——	.15	.35	.60	.60	.85
F	——	.25	.40	.90	1.40	1.40	1.50
XF	——	——	1.50	3.50	5.00	10.00	13.00
MS60	.50	1.50	5.00	16.50	40.00	——	——
MS63	——	——	——	——	——	125.00	75.00

Comments: 1929-D is similar to 1928-D in that well struck coins are scarce, and fully struck examples are very rare (in the coin shown, the strike is atypical). Unlike 1928-D, however, 1929-D does not provide such a large pool of coins from which to select. Some uncirculated pieces have very little of the horn showing, the head being not much more than an undefined mass.

Luster for this issue is average to good, with only a few really outstanding examples appearing. The typical coin has some roughness on the highpoints where the deficient strike failed to compress the metal enough to smooth out the planchet's original texture. This is typical of many nickels from the 1920s onward, whereas the earlier pieces were evidently struck from much smoother planchets. The planchets used during the 1910s were sometimes quite well polished, producing a charming prooflike quality to the more softly struck pieces.

Continuing the speculation begun with respect to 1928-D nickels, the 1929-D issue must have gone into circulation at or near the time of manufacture, as fewer are available in mint state. These were the last nickels coined at Denver until 1934, and they may have been released before the 1928-D pieces. This is consistent with the "last in-first out" theory of vault storage applicable at the mints and federal reserve banks. When demand for additional coinage resurfaces after years of dormancy, the most accessible coins are usually the last ones that were bagged and stored. Though a few dealers had rolls of 1929-D nickels available during the late 1930s and into the 1940s, these were greatly overshadowed by the abundance of 1928-D rolls.

1929-D nickels were among the coins that could be ordered from the Treasury Department, circa 1932. These listings of available coins were published as late as 1940, but it appears that the booming wartime economy eliminated both the reserve of unissued coins and the government's willingness to indulge collectors. It was not until 1948 that hobbyists were once again able to obtain uncirculated coins directly from the Treasury, when it began selling double sets of the previous year's coinage.

1929-S

Mintage:
7,754,000
(Ranking 29/64)

Popular Varieties:

Two repunched mintmark varieties are reported. In addition, a two-feathers variety is reported by Norm Talbert.

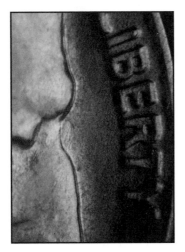

Strike doubling
(Vic Rollo)

Strike doubling
(Rollo)

RPM-1
(Tom Miller)

Rarity: 1929-S is the most common S-Mint nickel of the 1920s in all grades. Flashy AU coins, also known as "sliders", are common. While truly mint state examples are slightly scarce, a greater than usual proportion of these are choice. Gems, however, remain elusive. BU rolls of this date were frequently available from dealers during the 1930s, though they seem to have become well dispersed after that time.

RATINGS: G-VG R1, **F** R1, **VF** R1, **XF-AU** R2, **MS60-63** R2, **MS64** R2, **MS65** R3

TOTAL MS PCGS/NGC = 1189 (Ranking 38/64)

Values:

	1940	1950	1960	1970	1980	1990	2000
G	——	——	.15	.35	.55	.55	.75
F	——	.25	.40	.90	1.00	1.00	1.00
XF	——	——	1.25	3.50	4.00	7.00	8.00
MS60	.35	1.25	4.50	16.50	30.00	——	——
MS63	——	——	——	——	——	90.00	70.00

Comments: Though a fairly large number of examples have been certified as MS65, this grading does not take into account the quality of strike. Flashy coins having mediocre detail are common for this date and probably account for most of these "gems."

The greater than expected availability of this date in grades XF-AU suggests hoarding by collectors. Perhaps, like 1930-S and 1931-S, many of these coins went into storage during the Depression that began in 1929. Released much later, circa 1934-35, they may have been set aside after only a brief period of circulation. The introduction of inexpensive coin boards for collectors dates from this period and would have provided additional incentive to retain these coins.

1929-S nickels were among the coins that could be ordered from the Treasury Department at face value, plus postage, circa 1932.

1930

Mintage:
22,849,000
(Ranking 47/64)

Popular Varieties:

There are at least six doubled-die obverse varieties for this issue, though most are trivial. The most desirable one shows doubling at the date and the Indian's nostril and eyelid (B-2639, FS-017).

The several doubled-die reverses known are mostly shallow and difficult to discern. The best of these is FS-017.5, popularly known as the 5-leg variety. Two others are also included within *The Cherrypickers' Guide to Rare Die Varieties* (FS-017.3, FS-017.4).

DDO-1
(Van Allen)

DDO-1
(Van Allen)

DDO-2
(Van Allen)

DDR-1
(Fivaz/Stanton)

DDR-2
(Van Allen)

Rarity: 1930-P nickels are common in all grades including gem mint state. Original rolls likely exist.

RATINGS: G-VG R1, **F** R1, **VF** R1, **XF-AU** R2, **MS60-63** R2, **MS64** R2, **MS65** R3

TOTAL MS PCGS/NGC = 1858 (Ranking 49/64)

Values:

	1940	1950	1960	1970	1980	1990	2000
G	—	—	—	.35	.40	.40	.75
F	—	.10	.15	.65	.85	.85	1.00
XF	—	—	.75	2.00	4.00	4.00	4.00
MS60	.50	1.50	4.00	14.00	25.00	—	—
MS63	—	—	—	—	—	65.00	40.00

Comments: Most 1930-P nickels have just average to good strikes, though they frequently possess really dazzling luster. The careful buyer will hold out for a well struck examples, as there are many uncirculated coins from which to select.

The suggestion that some examples of this date feature a larger than normal LIBERTY is without merit, as a single master die was used throughout the year. More likely is that extended use of a particular obverse die caused the legend to become distorted through erosion. Normal die life for nickels was about 150,000 to 300,000 impressions, but the decision to remove an old die or to continue using it was made at the discretion of the coiner and the die setter.

This was the last mintage of nickels at Philadelphia until 1934. The Great Depression resulted in such slow commercial activity that there was little or no demand for additional coins during 1931-33.

1930-P nickels were among the coins that could be ordered from the Treasury Department, circa 1932. It's probable that the government was making these coins available in response to complaints from collectors that recent dates had not been released to banks. This issue really came to a head in 1932 when collectors pleaded that cents of that date be made available. There existed virtually no demand from banks for additional coins, and the cents of both 1932 and 1933 were scarce at the time. Released a year or two later, vast numbers went directly into the hands of speculators, and they remain common in uncirculated condition to this day.

1930-S

Mintage:
5,435,000
(Ranking 17/64)

Popular Varieties:

Two repunched mintmark varieties have been found. The more desirable of these is RPM-2, FS-017.71.

A two-feathers variety is also known (FS-017.711). No examples of this class of variety have been seen dated later than 1930, but the reason for this is unknown. The three United States Mints may have become more particular about discarding damaged dies, but the 3-1/2 leg variety of 1936 and the 3 leg variety of 1937 suggest that at the Denver Mint it remained business as usual.

Rarity:

1930-S is a fairly common date in all grades through choice uncirculated. It is only slightly scarce in gem condition, if one is not particular about the quality of strike.
RATINGS: G-VG R1, **F** R1, **VF** R2, **XF-AU** R2, **MS60-63** R2, **MS64** R2, **MS65** R3
TOTAL MS PCGS/NGC = 927 (Ranking 30/64)

Values:

	1940	1950	1960	1970	1980	1990	2000
G	——	——	.30	.60	.50	.50	.75
F	——	.30	1.00	1.60	1.00	1.00	1.00
XF	——	——	2.00	5.50	5.75	6.75	7.00
MS60	.40	2.50	10.00	40.00	50.00	——	——
MS63	——	——	——	——	——	125.00	75.00

Comments:

Incomplete strikes are the norm for this date, though fully struck pieces are occasionally available from among the relatively high percentage of mint state survivors. The typical 1930-S nickel has good to excellent luster, and this probably accounts for the large number of pieces certified as gems.

1930-S nickels were among the coins that could be ordered directly from the Treasury Department, circa 1932, at face value plus postage. This is a date that was largely withheld from release at the time of manufacture, as little demand existed for new coinage during the Depression. Placed into storage, these were still on hand in 1934 when the economy first began to recover. Upon their release, these low mintage coins were quickly hoarded by speculators and dealers residing in the West, most notably Norman Shultz. Sold at retail via mail orders or parceled out to other dealers in small lots, they have been fairly common ever since. The availability of so many mint state examples has depressed the value of circulated pieces.

RPM-1
(Norm Talbert)

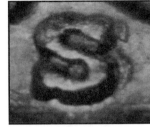

RPM-2
(Tom Miller)

1931-S

Mintage:
1,200,000
(Ranking 2/64)

Popular Varieties:

Probably the most desirable variety is the repunched mintmark.

Minor die doubling is reported for the reverse.

Also known is a small cud affecting the bison right hind leg, a very unusual location for such failure.

RPM-1
(Talbert)

Rarity:

This date is scarce in low grades, yet abundant in mint state. While most examples are not fully struck, choice and gem pieces are nevertheless fairly common. Original rolls almost certainly still exist.

As testimony to this issue's availability in mint state, several hoards of varying size have turned up. Perhaps the largest accumulation of uncirculated pieces was dispersed by [Terry] Hathaway and [Q. David] Bowers Galleries during 1969-70. Some 2,476 1931-S nickels, all described as "Gem BU," were offered in quantities ranging from the single piece to rolls of 40 coins.

RATINGS: G-VG R3, **F** R2, **VF** R2, **XF-AU** R2, **MS60-63** R2, **MS64** R2, **MS65** R2

TOTAL MS PCGS/NGC = 2749 (Ranking 58/64)

Values:

	1940	1950	1960	1970	1980	1990	2000
G	——	——	.60	4.25	3.50	3.50	3.50
F	——	.30	1.25	6.00	5.50	5.50	5.50
XF	——	——	3.50	15.00	10.00	10.00	10.00
MS60	.30	2.50	9.50	60.00	62.50	——	——
MS63	——	——	——	——	——	125.00	65.00

Comments:

Although many specimens are softly struck, the sheer number of mint state coins available makes it fairly easy to find a satisfying example. The typical 1931-S nickel has excellent luster, and some are blazing beauties. Since the coin market typically places so little emphasis on technical matters such as die state and quality of strike, there are a great many examples of this issue carrying high grades.

1931-S is to the Buffalo Nickel series what 1950-D is to the Jefferson Nickels. It seems to be at least as common in mint state as it is in lesser grades, possibly more so. As a low mintage date, speculators were attracted to it from the outset. That their scheme could be implemented successfully was due primarily to a delay of several years before the majority of 1931-S nickels were released. With the economy at such a slow pace, new coins were simply not needed. When things finally did pick up, around 1934, sufficient time had passed for this issue's low mintage figure to become public knowledge, and the trap was set.

The mintage of this date would have been lower still, had not steps been taken to increase it. Researcher R. W. Julian turned up a letter that explains exactly what happened. Dated November 19, 1931, it was written by Acting Director of the Mint M. M. O'Reilly to the superintendent of the San Francisco Mint:

> The only nickels coined this year were those manufactured at your mint; $9,700 worth being issued in January. This amount, if allowed to be the total coinage for the year, would send the nickels of 1931 to a premium and would cause the Treasurer and this Bureau a good deal of trouble for years. This Bureau has conferred with the Treasurer's Office and it is suggested that you discontinue the coinage of dimes and prepare to run on nickels for the balance of the calendar year.
>
> It is understood that you have about $14,700 worth of nickels for recoinage and that you have in addition a sufficient amount of nickel on hand to permit you to continue coining this denomination until the close of the calendar year. This Bureau will be glad to have you manufacture as many of these coins as you can without overtime. After the beginning of the calendar year 1932, it is suggested that you resume the coinage of dimes and one-cent pieces.[10]

So, were it not for the diligence of bureaucrats in Washington, the mintage of 1931-S nickels would have been limited to 194,000 pieces! No amount of hoarding would have prevented this from becoming a scarce and expensive coin. As things turned out, though it's likely to remain a popular date with collectors, the 1931-S nickel offers an uncertain prospect for investors. This is evident from its price history, which has been deservedly lackluster during the past twenty years.

The second suggestion of Acting Director O'Reilly, that cents and dimes be struck in 1932, was not followed, and 1931-S proved to be the last coinage of nickels at San Francisco until 1935. Though they were not released in quantity until a few years later, 1931-S nickels were among the coins that could be ordered directly from the Treasury Department at face value plus postage. Speculators were discouraged, however, as a two-coin limit was placed on each order.

1934

Mintage:
20,213,003
(Ranking 43/64)

Popular Varieties:

A doubled-die reverse was discovered by Leroy and Marilyn Van Allen and published in *Coin World* some years ago.

Rarity:

1934-P is fairly common in all grades through the lower levels of mint state. Choice and gem examples are not always available. Original rolls likely exist.

RATINGS: **G-VG** R1, **F** R1, **VF** R1, **XF-AU** R2, **MS60-63** R2, **MS64** R3, **MS65** R3

TOTAL MS PCGS/NGC = 1109 (Ranking 36/64)

Values:

	1940	1950	1960	1970	1980	1990	2000
G	——	——	——	.25	.30	.30	.75
F	——	——	.25	.65	.60	.60	1.00
XF	——	——	.75	2.00	3.50	3.50	4.00
MS60	.35	1.25	3.75	11.00	26.00	——	——
MS63	——	——	——	——	——	60.00	35.00

Comments:

The strike on most seen is not as sharp as for other P-Mint issues of the 1930s, and the quality of luster varies from good to excellent. Still, by virtue of the sheer number of mint state coins available, a satisfactory example can be found with a bit of patience.

This was the first coinage of nickels at the Philadelphia Mint since 1930. Economic recovery was still more of a hope than a reality, but spending by the federal government made up part of the deficiency in the commercial sector.

1934-D

Mintage:
7,480,000
(Ranking 26/64)

Popular Varieties:

Two minor doubled-die reverse varieties are known, as is a repunched mintmark.

Most examples seen have the Large D mintmark first used on the cents of 1933, but a minority of this date feature the Small D of 1917-29. These were evidently struck using reverse dies leftover from previous years.

Rarity:

Common in low grades, coins grading VF through AU are elusive due to poor strikes. Mint state coins are usually available, with choice pieces being scarce and fully struck gems exceedingly rare. This issue is the key to completing the popular "short set" of 1934-38.

RATINGS: G-VG R1, **F** R1, **VF** R2, **XF-AU** R3, **MS60-63** R2, MS64, R3, **MS65** R4

TOTAL MS PCGS/NGC = 1595 (Ranking 46/64)

Values:

	1940	1950	1960	1970	1980	1990	2000
G	——	——	——	.30	.45	.45	.75
F	——	——	.45	.70	.85	.85	1.00
XF	——	——	1.25	2.50	5.00	5.00	8.00
MS60	.35	1.50	4.75	13.50	32.00	——	——
MS63	——	——	——	——	——	115.00	70.00

Comments:

Weak strikes are the rule for this date, though the symptoms are not as severe as for coins of the 1920s. Locating a well struck coin is nevertheless very challenging. Luster for the 1934-D nickel is just average to good. The highpoints are often marred by areas of uncompressed planchet, the metal's original texture contrasting unattractively with the more finished areas of the coin. Note that the example illustrated has a mint-made planchet void above the bison's foreleg.

This issue represents the first coinage of nickels by the Denver Mint since 1929! The Midwest was hit hardest by the Great Depression, feeling its effects even before the stock market crash of October 1929. When production of nickels resumed in the latter part of 1934, these pieces appear to have been released almost concurrently with much of the 1926-D, 1928-D and 1929-D mintage. Speculators hoarded the earlier dates, while permitting the 1934-D nickels to become relatively scarce in uncirculated condition.

1935

Mintage:
58,264,000
(Ranking 59/64)

Popular Varieties:

The most desirable variety for this date is the spectacular doubled-die reverse (B-2644, DDR-1, FS-018). The combined PCGS/NGC population for this variety is 3 MS and 20 circulated.

A less dramatic doubled-die reverse is also known (FS-018.1), but its value is much lower.

The 2-leg nickels of this date occasionally seen are contemporary counterfeits.[11]

Finally, this date is a rich hunting ground for cud breaks. In addition to the bison's familiar cap, another variety is known with the letters TS in CENTS obliterated.

DDR-1
(Fivaz/Stanton)

DDR-1
(Fivaz/Stanton)

Rarity: 1935-P is common in all grades. Original rolls likely exist.
RATINGS: G-VG R1, **F** R1, **VF** R1, **XF-AU** R1, **MS60-63** R1, **MS64** R1, **MS65** R2
TOTAL MS PCGS/NGC = 1749 (Ranking 48/64)

Values:

	1940	1950	1960	1970	1980	1990	2000
G	——	——	——	——	.30	.30	.75
F	——	——	.15	.35	.45	.45	1.00
XF	——	——	.35	1.10	2.00	2.25	2.25
MS60	.25	.50	1.25	5.50	20.00	——	——
MS63	——	——	——	——	——	35.00	20.00

Comments: Some examples are weak in the central obverse, but well struck coins are available. A particularly severe example of weak striking for this issue is illustrated in Chapter 5.

1935-P is another coin for which luster varies dramatically from one piece to the next. Even so, there are quite a large number displaying really outstanding luster, which is almost always of a frosty texture. As is often the case with Buffalo Nickels, the most lustrous coins seem to be a bit softly struck, while the really sharp examples have more muted luster.

A single coin described as a "specimen" striking has been reported but is presently unconfirmed (see Chapter 7).

1935-D

Mintage:
12,092,000
(Ranking 39/64)

Popular Varieties:

Three repunched mintmark varieties are known, including one punched at least four times (FS-018.5).

A cud break is known for the reverse.

RPM-1
(Miller)

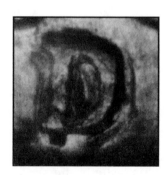

D/D/D/D (FS-018.5)
(Fivaz/Stanton)

D/D/D
(Miller)

D/D
(Talbert)

Rarity: 1935-D is common in the lower circulated grades and in the lower range of mint state. XF-AU coins are scarce, because the striking quality was such that most pieces went straight from uncirculated to VF while still retaining luster. Choice and gem examples are obtainable, but only if one discounts the importance of strike. Fully-struck gems are genuinely rare.

RATINGS: **G-VG** R1, **F** R1, **VF** R2, **XF-AU** R3, **MS60-63** R2, **MS64** R3, **MS65** R4

TOTAL MS PCGS/NGC = 1543 (Ranking 45/64)

Values:

	1940	1950	1960	1970	1980	1990	2000
G	——	——	——	——	.35	.35	.75
F	——	——	.20	.50	.60	.60	1.25
XF	——	——	.75	2.00	3.50	3.50	8.00
MS60	.40	.75	2.50	10.50	22.50	——	——
MS63	——	——	——	——	——	110.00	50.00

Comments: 1935-D is the last date in the series for which weak striking is a serious obstacle to locating a satisfactory example. Many of these coins were struck from extremely worn dies showing heavy erosion lines. While a bit of die wear actually enhances the coin's luster, giving it the familiar frosty texture, extreme die erosion diffuses the reflected light so much that the result is unsatisfying. This describes the typical 1935-D nickel.

This issue is the second scarcest coin in the popular "short set" of 1934-38. Collecting the Buffalo Nickel series in its entirety is an expensive proposition for the collector seeking only mint state coins, but this 12-piece alternative to a complete set is an attainable goal.

1935-S

Mintage:
10,300,000
(Ranking 36/64)

Popular Varieties:

Six repunched mintmark varieties are illustrated in *The RPM Book* by John Wexler and Tom Miller and no less than eleven in Wexler's *Treasure Hunting Buffalo Nickels,* co-authored with Ron Pope and Kevin Flynn.

A minor doubled-die reverse is also known for this issue (FS-018.6).

Rarity:

1935-S nickels are common in all grades through choice mint state. Gems are a little more challenging, as most coins of this date are not fully struck. Since grading services do not place much emphasis on strike, the number of certified gems is thus a bit misleading. Original rolls likely exist.

RATINGS: G-VG R1, **F** R1, **VF** R1, **XF-AU** R2, **MS60-63** R1, **MS64** R2, **MS65** R3

TOTAL MS PCGS/NGC = 2028 (Ranking 53/64)

Values:

	1940	1950	1960	1970	1980	1990	2000
G	——	——	——	——	.35	.35	.75
F	——	——	.25	.50	.50	.50	1.00
XF	——	——	.90	1.90	2.50	2.50	2.50
MS60	.35	.75	3.00	9.75	22.00	——	——
MS63	——	——	——	——	——	50.00	35.00

Comments:

Most 1935-S nickels are not fully struck, though it's less of a problem than for the Denver nickels of this date.

Most examples have good to outstanding luster. The real trick to finding the optimal specimen is seeking a coin that has both great luster and a sharp impression. Such pieces are truly rare.

The large number of repunched mintmark dies used during 1934-38 was likely due to the increased demand for coinage after several fallow years. To meet this demand the Philadelphia Mint's engraving department took on a number of new employees. The existence of so many clumsily prepared dies suggests that the

DDR-1
(Van Allen)

RPM-1
(Miller)

RPM-2
(Fivaz/Stanton)

RPM-3
(Miller)

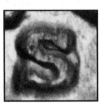

RPM-4
(Miller)

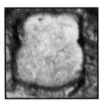

RPM-5
(Miller)

1936

Mintage:
119,001,420
(Ranking 64/64)

Popular Varieties:

One obverse doubled die is known, but it's evident only as extra thickness in the date and LIBERTY (DDO-1, FS-018.7).

A quite similar variety may be found for the reverse (FS-018.8).

At least one cud break is also known for the reverse. This is in the commonly seen location that gives the bison the appearance of wearing a cap.

Walter Breen's listing of a three-and-a-half leg variety is in error. He was evidently thinking of the similar variety known for 1936-D.

Rarity:

This is the highest mintage date in the series, and it remains among the most common issues in all grades. Original rolls probably exist.

RATINGS: G-VG R1, **F** R1, **VF** R1, **XF-AU** R1, **MS60-63** R1, **MS64** R1, **MS65** R1

TOTAL MS PCGS/NGC = 3095
(Ranking 59/64)

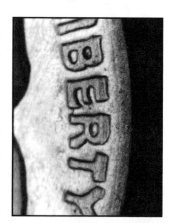

DDO-1
(Fivaz/Stanton)

Values:

	1940	1950	1960	1970	1980	1990	2000
G	—	—	—	—	.30	.30	.75
F	—	—	—	.30	.40	.40	1.00
XF	—	—	.35	.65	1.50	2.25	2.25
MS60	.25	.50	1.25	4.50	18.00	—	—
MS63	—	—	—	—	—	25.00	20.00

Comments:

The quality of strike varies from average to excellent for this issue. It appears that most coins were made from properly set dies, but these dies were permitted to wear until they became quite distorted by erosion. With such an abundance of mint state coins for this issue it should be little challenge to find one that is both highly lustrous and fully struck.

A number of die-struck counterfeits are known of this date and were made from the same reverse die used for the 1935 two-legged nickels.[12] The dies themselves may have been cast. For an example, see Chapter 4.

1936-D

Mintage:
24,814,000
(Ranking 49/64)

Popular Varieties:

Seven repunched mintmark varieties are illustrated in Wexler/Miller, including two that are triple punched. One of the most popular D/D varieties is FS-019.5. The D/D/S variety (FS-019.8) is controversial. I, for one, don't believe that it includes an S mintmark.

A 3-1/2-leg variety is known that shows the bison's right foreleg partially removed through excessive die polishing (B-2647, FS-019). For a more detailed explanation of this phenomenon, see 1937-D.

RPM-1
(Miller)

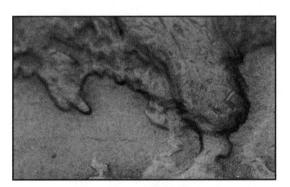

Three-and-a-half legged variety
(Fivaz/Stanton)

RPM-2
(Miller)

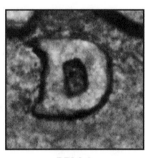

RPM-3
(Miller)

RPM-4
(Miller)

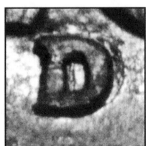

D/D/D RPM-5
(Miller)

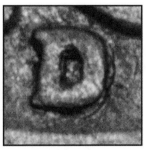

RPM-6
(Miller)

RPM-7
(Miller)

Rarity: 1936-D nickels are somewhat challenging to locate in gem due to incomplete striking. However, enough have been certified to meet the demand. Original rolls likely
exist.

RATINGS: G-VG R1, **F** R1, **VF** R1, **XF-AU** R1, **MS60-63** R1, **MS64** R1, **MS65** R2

TOTAL MS PCGS/NGC = 2032 (Ranking 54/64)

Values:

	1940	1950	1960	1970	1980	1990	2000
G	——	——	——	——	.30	.30	.75
F	——	——	——	.40	.50	.50	1.00
XF	——	——	.35	1.15	2.00	2.25	2.50
MS60	.25	.60	1.25	4.75	20.00	——	——
MS63	——	——	——	——	——	35.00	22.00

Comments: 1936-D nickels are generally quite superior to the two Denver Mint issues that pre-
ceded them. While some are not fully struck, there are enough nice ones to meet
the needs of the more discriminating collectors. Luster is typically very good to outstanding for this date.

As with all of the Buffalo Nickels from the late 1930s, this issue is sometimes subject
to planchet flaws. When mintages increase as much as they did during this time
period, the mints became less careful with both the planchets made in-house and
those ordered from contractors.

This may be a good place to recall that prior to 1996 all dies were manufactured at
the Philadelphia Mint, while their final preparation and in-use maintenance has
always been the responsibility of each individual facility. Therefore, repunched
mintmarks and doubled dies within the Buffalo Nickel series are traceable to
Philadelphia. Die clashing, and the overpolishing which often results from
attempts to remove clash marks, are attributable to the mint at which a particular
coin was struck.

1936-S

Mintage:
14,930,000
(Ranking 41/64)

Popular Varieties:

Two repunched mintmark varieties are known. One of these (FS-020) is a naked-eye variety and perhaps the most obvious such RPM in the Buffalo Nickel series.

Rarity:

1936-S nickels are common in all grades including gem. Original rolls likely exist.
RATINGS: G-VG R1, **F** R1, **VF** R1, **XF-AU** R1, **MS60-63** R1, **MS64** R1, **MS65** R2
TOTAL MS PCGS/NGC = 2193 (56/64)

Values:

	1940	1950	1960	1970	1980	1990	2000
G	——	——	——	——	.30	.30	.75
F	——	——	——	.40	.50	.50	1.00
XF	——	——	.45	1.20	1.90	2.25	2.25
MS60	.25	.70	1.50	5.50	20.00	——	——
MS63	——	——	——	——	——	37.50	20.00

Comments:

The 1936-S nickel almost always comes well struck and pleasingly lustrous. Some are satiny, but the vast majority have luster that is frosty.

This date was widely hoarded by the roll. Banks in the western states were still releasing these coins in 1938 when it was announced that the Buffalo Nickel would soon be replaced. The saving of rolls had first become popular around 1933-34, on the heels of several low-mintage dates in each denomination. By the late 1930s, this practice was a familiar ritual to thousands of collectors and speculators, and it is to them that modern collectors owe the abundance of BU coins dated 1934 and later.

Given the number of repunched mintmarks for 1936-D and other branch mint nickels of this era, it's likely that more varieties will be found for this date.

RPM-1, FS-020
(Miller)

RPM-2
(Miller)

1937

Mintage:
79,485,769
(Ranking 63/64)

Popular Varieties:

None are reported aside from the whimsical reeded edge coins (see Comments).

Rarity:

As befits its high mintage, this is the second most common date in the series. Examples are readily available in all grades. 1937-P is the most available Philadelphia Mint Buffalo Nickel in gem condition. Original rolls probably exist.

RATINGS: G-VG R1, **F** R1, **VF** R1, **XF-AU** R1, **MS60-63** R1, **MS64** R1, **MS65** R1

TOTAL MS PCGS/NGC = 9560 (Ranking 63/64)

Values:

	1940	1950	1960	1970	1980	1990	2000
G	—	—	—	—	.30	.30	.75
F	—	—	—	.30	.45	.45	1.00
XF	—	—	.30	.70	1.50	2.25	2.00
MS60	.15	.35	.75	4.25	18.00	—	—
MS63	—	—	—	—	—	23.00	18.00

Comments:

This date is typically found with very good to excellent luster. Most often seen are frosty, textured coins, but many satiny or semi-prooflike pieces survive from early states of the dies. Fully struck examples are easy to locate, though most examples will show varying degrees of die erosion. Such large mintages were obtained only through long press runs, and the dies were simply not changed as quickly as they should have been. Note the extreme sharpness of the piece illustrated. From the photographs alone it might pass for a proof, yet the flatness in the outermost feather gives it away as a currency strike.

When the demise of the Buffalo Nickel was announced, early in 1938, a scramble began to hoard uncirculated examples. As no coins of this type were struck at Philadelphia that year, 1937-P became the principal target of opportunity for collectors in the East. It has been common ever since.

Some 1937-P nickels are found with a reeded edge. Though the coins themselves are genuine, the reeding was applied outside of the mint. These do not represent a legitimate variety, but rather are novelty coins. Philadelphia coin dealer Ira Reed reportedly had 104 sets of 1937 cents and nickels reeded at a machine shop for the

1941 convention of the ANA, held in that city (the reeding was a play on his name). These coins were either presented to friends or sold at four dollars per set, according to Lee F. Hewitt, editor of *The Numismatic Scrapbook Magazine* (coin dealer Milferd Bolender reported a price of five dollars per set).

Ira Reed's whimsical novelty, the 1937 reeded edge nickel
(Talbert)

Although these coins may have some value as souvenirs of the convention, the premium attached to them is limited because such reeding can be applied to additional coins at any time. An exception would be a coin that can be conclusively linked to the convention.

1937-D

Mintage:
17,826,000
(Ranking 42/64)

Popular Varieties:

One of the most well known and popular varieties in this or any series is the 1937-D 3-legged buffalo. It was discovered early on and has captured the imagination of coin hunters ever since. Inclusion in the Red Book (*A Guide Book of United States Coins*) and most coin albums has secured its place on collectors' want lists.

Five repunched mintmark varieties are illustrated in Wexler/Miller, with one being triple punched. Breen lists a possible D/S variety (B-2653), but this remains in dispute. It is alternatively described as D/D or D/D/S.

Rarity:

1937-D nickels are common in all grades. Original rolls likely exist.

RATINGS: **G-VG** R1, **F** R1, **VF** R1, **XF-AU** R1, **MS60-63** R1, **MS64** R1, **MS65** R2

TOTAL MS PCGS/NGC = 4671 (Ranking 61/64)

Values:

	1940	1950	1960	1970	1980	1990	2000
G	——	——	——	——	.30	.30	.75
F	——	——	——	.40	.55	.55	1.00
XF	——	——	.35	1.00	1.75	2.25	2.00
MS60	.25	.40	1.00	5.00	20.00	——	——
MS63	——	——	——	——	——	25.00	19.00

Comments:

An abundance of mint state pieces from the many hoarded rolls means that a bit of selective shopping will turn up an ideal specimen. Most 1937-D nickels have very good to excellent luster that is typically frosty.

D/S or D/D?
(David Blasczak)

The dies for this issue were used far too long, and they reveal light to very heavy erosion. The latter is seen most prominently of the 3-leg variety. While coins struck from eroded dies are unappealing to me, the coin market does not place much emphasis on die state, and such coins can sometimes receive very high grades on account of their good luster.

RPM-1a
(Miller)

RPM-1b
(Miller)

RPM-2
(Miller)

RPM-3
(Miller)

RPM-4
(Miller)

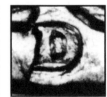
RPM-5
(Talbert)

1937-D
Three-Legged Variety

Rarity: Mint state coins are scarce but sometimes available. They turn up at coin shows less often than their certified population would suggest, due to an unceasing demand. Choice examples are scarce, gems rare. Most pieces encountered grade VF-AU. This is not surprising, as the discovery of this variety was announced within a few years of issue. Low grade specimens are somewhat scarce.

RATINGS: **G-VG** R4, **F** R3, **VF** R2, **XF-AU** R3, **MS60-63** R3, **MS64** R4, **MS65** R6

TOTAL MS PCGS/NGC = 1079

TOTAL CIRCULATED PCGS/NGC = 2670

Values:

	1950	1960	1970	1980	1990	2000
G	1.25	8.00	35.00	70.00	80.00	140.00
F	2.00	15.00	48.00	90.00	125.00	250.00
XF	——	25.00	80.00	125.00	250.00	450.00
MS60	7.50	42.50	220.00	600.00	——	——
MS63	——	——	——	——	1,500.00	3,000.00

Comments: Most mint state examples have just so-so luster, since the eroded state of the dies resulted in coins having very diffused light reflection. Examples having bright and pleasing luster are quite rare.

This die-polishing variety was the first of its kind to capture the imagination of collectors, though several similar but less dramatic examples have since turned up for other dates.

This variety was evidently discovered by, or at least first publicized by, C. L. "Cowboy" Franzen. He was advertising them for sale in *The Numismatic Scrapbook Magazine* as early as 1937-38.

The distribution of 1937-D three-legged nickels seems to have occurred in Montana. Evidence for this is provided in a letter to the editor of *The Numismatic Scrapbook Magazine* written by veteran coin dealer Aubrey Bebee. He was writing in response to an earlier submission, as noted in the following:

Maurice Gould is undoubtedly correct in his assumption that Montana was the main "stamping ground" of the 3-legged Buffaloes. While touring the West for several months in 1939, we stopped at Bozeman, Montana, for several days, where Mrs. Bebee and I had the great pleasure of meeting Harold C. White, who informed us of the existence of this freak. I bought several of these nickels from Mr. White, as I doubted that I would be able to find any as late as 1939. However, the next day I went to the banks there and from four $50.00 bags found about 30 specimens. In Great Falls, Montana, we did not find as many but here we found several that were strictly uncirculated. Two months later, we returned from Canada and toured Idaho, Washington, Oregon and other western states, and the only 3-legged Buffaloes we found were in the possession of collectors.[13]

When coin collecting was at its peak of popularity during the late 1950s and early 1960s, this variety was frequently falsified from regular 1937-D nickels by grinding off the bison's leg (see Chapter 4). Such work was usually crude, and it can easily be detected by persons armed with a few facts. Genuine examples were struck from just a single pair of dies. The reverse die features several diagnostic points, the most distinctive of which is a stream of raised lumps between the front and hind legs, curving from the ground to the top of the left rear leg. These lumps are caused by rust pits in the die, which was already overdue for retirement. Also look for a pointed beard on the bison with its right tip longer than the left, rear legs that are thin and rough and a bison that is slightly smaller overall than on the normal 1937-D. Other signs of extreme die fatigue are heavy metal flow lines in the bison's back, rump and hind legs, as well as inside the reverse borders.

This variety was caused by excessive polishing of the dies to remove clash marks. Die clash occurs when the feeder mechanism of a coin press fails to deliver a planchet, the dies strike one another, and each receives an impression of the opposing die. This disfigurement, when discovered, usually results in the replacement of both dies. In the case of the 1937-D 3-legged nickel, however, the urgency of completing a coinage run precluded this customary practice, and a swifter solution was sought.

Breen recounts that one of the newly hired coiners, a Mr. Young, applied an emery stick to the dies in an effort to grind off the evidence of clashing. In so doing he also removed the element of lowest relief in the die, the bison's right foreleg between hoof and thigh. This went unnoticed until the coins had already been distributed to banks. Such deliveries were reportedly made in Montana, most examples coming from that part of the country. This account helps to explain why so few uncirculated examples are known, coin collectors being equally scarce in that part of the country.

1937-S

Mintage:
5,635,000
(Ranking 18/64)

Popular Varieties:

Four repunched mintmark varieties are included in Wexler/Miller, and two of these are illustrated here. More are likely to be discovered.

A retained cud die break is known for the reverse and affects the word CENTS. A completed break of this same die may also exist.

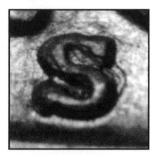

S/S/S RPM-1
(Miller)

RPM-2b
(Miller)

RPM-3
(Miller)

Rarity:

This issue is common in all grades. It is also the most available S-Mint Buffalo Nickel in gem condition. Original rolls likely exist.

RATINGS: G-VG R1, **F** R1, **VF** R1, **XF-AU** R1, **MS60-63** R1, **MS64** R1, **MS65** R2

TOTAL MS PCGS/NGC = 3977 (Ranking 60/64)

Values:

	1940	1950	1960	1970	1980	1990	2000
G	——	——	——	——	.40	.40	.75
F	——	——	——	.50	.55	.55	1.00
XF	——	——	.35	1.30	1.75	2.25	2.00
MS60	.25	.50	1.25	6.25	20.00	——	——
MS63	——	——	——	——	——	25.00	19.00

Comments: Well struck coins are abundant, and some of them are extremely sharp. Nearly all 1937-S nickels have very good to outstanding luster, and this ranges all the way from semi-prooflike to satiny, to frosty.

This was the last coinage of Buffalo Nickels at the San Francisco Mint, and examples were widely hoarded as such. The fact that these coins were still being released a year or two later enabled speculators to put away countless rolls.

An interesting item from the January 1939 issue of *The Numismatic Scrapbook Magazine* tells something about the circulation of these coins at the time. In his column "From California," correspondent Roy Hill noted the failure of the new Jefferson Nickel to supplant its predecessor:

> The closing months of 1938 have brought into circulation here more new coins dated 1938, including the Washington quarters. Now our change is checkered with bright cents, dimes and nickels. The nickels are either 1936 or 1937 and it is interesting to note their "color" which is sometimes a clear nickel and then again it seems to have a "tint".
>
> Those 1938 Jefferson's are still elusive–most banks having scant supplies and releasing but two or so to a person. None have been picked up in trade channels. I started one on its way but doubt if it got very far. People, who wouldn't ordinarily be interested in the money they handle catch it right away and comments heard in stores confirm the idea they have to hang on to them – lest they prove rare.

1938-D

Mintage:
7,020,000
(Ranking 25/64)

Popular Varieties:

A cherrypicker's dream, the 1938-D Buffalo Nickel is known with three repunched D varieties and no less than five overmintmark D/S varieties. Of the latter, one is D/D/S, while a second is D/D/D/S (FS-020.5).

RPM-1
(Talbert)

RPM-2
(Miller)

RPM-3
(Miller)

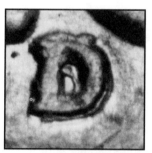

D/D/D/S OMM-1
(Miller)

D/D/S OMM-1b
(Miller)

D/S OMM-2
(Miller)

D/S OMM-3a
(Miller)

D/S OMM-3b
(Miller)

D/S OMM-4
(Miller)

Rarity: As the only issue from the final year of production, 1938-D Buffalo Nickels were widely saved in mint state. Although slightly scarce in lower circulated grades, AU and uncirculated coins are exceedingly common.

RATINGS: **G-VG** R2, **F** R2, **VF** R1, **XF-AU** R1, **MS60-63** R1, **MS64** R1, **MS65** R1

Total MS PCGS/NGC = 47,028 (Ranking 64/64)

Total MS PCGS/NGC for D/S = 2641 (includes all varieties)

Values:

	1940	1950	1960	1970	1980	1990	2000
G	——	——	——	——	.40	.40	.75
F	——	——	——	.45	.55	.55	1.00
XF	——	——	.25	1.25	1.75	2.25	2.00
MS60	.25	.25	.75	4.75	17.50	——	——
MS63	——	——	——	——	——	23.00	18.00

Comments: This date is the quintessential type coin. Almost always well struck, 1938-D nickels were hoarded by the thousands of rolls. Most mint state examples are choice to gem, and even the D/D and D/S varieties are fairly common in gem condition.

This issue comprised the last emission of Buffalo Nickels from any of the United States Mints. The Associated Press ran a news item from Denver dated June 15 announcing the end of an era:

> "That's the last of the buffaloes," Mark A. Skinner, superintendent of the United States mint here, remarked as he broke up the casts [dies?] used in manufacturing 350,000 buffalo nickels. Skinner is awaiting arrival of new dies for the Jefferson model nickel.[14]

It was known early in 1938 that no more Buffalo Nickels would be coined after that year. What remained uncertain is whether the Philadelphia and San Francisco Mints would produce any. In his column "Capital Comment," Washington correspondent Harry X Boosel reprinted a mimeographed flyer issued by the Treasury Department in response to ceaseless inquiries about these coins:

> BUFFALO nickels of 1938 have been coined only by the United States Mint in Denver. Collectors may obtain one or two specimens thereof from the Treasurer of the United States, Washington, D. C. It is not expected that 1938 Buffalo nickels will be coined by the United States Mints in Philadelphia and San Francisco.[15]

Once minted, the 1938-D Buffalo Nickels were slow to appear in circulation, perhaps due to what was already widespread hoarding. Writing "From California," columnist Roy Hill remarked, "Recently some 1938 Denver nickels dribbled into circulation here, but lately none have been picked up. There are plenty of 1936 'S' to be found, but no 1937 as yet."[16]

Another account of the enthusiasm greeting the 1938-D Buffaloes was published in the newsletter of the Chicago Coin Club and summarized by Harry X Boosel, who noted that "$500 worth of them were received by the Loop banks and they were being passed out two at a time and it was necessary to sign your name and give your address." Boosel went on to observe that, "Usually only Philadelphia coins are available at the Treasury bank in the Treasury Building, but this time the Denver nickels are obtainable in rolls at the windows. Not more than two are furnished by the Treasury thru the mails, although they should be available later on thruout the country at most all banks."[17]

The fact that no coinage of Buffalo Nickels occurred at the San Francisco Mint clearly suggests that several S-mintmarked dies were deliberately repunched with a D mintmark for rerouting to the Denver Mint. Apparently, this was not achieved without some difficulty, as the multiple punchings reveal. The variety on which the undertype S is most clearly visible is the D/D/D/S (photo). Of the several varieties known, it is the only one that carries a measurable premium.

Before the subtle distinctions were made between its five varieties, the 1938-D/S nickel was already popular with collectors. It was the only overmintmark then known for a United States coin (a 1900-O/CC silver dollar reported early in the century had long since been forgotten). Discovered in 1961 by Robert Kerr and C. G. Langworthy, the two submitted it to *Coin World*. At the newspaper's request, its authenticity was then confirmed by Q. David Bowers. As with all newly-found varieties, it was initially proclaimed to be rare. Subsequent discoveries of hundreds of specimens proved otherwise. Even so, the publicity that the 1938-D/S nickels received launched a generation of variety collectors.

Footnotes to Chapter 6

[1] Horwitz, Edward S. "The Buffalo Nickel"

[2] *The Numismatist*, October 1918

[3] *The Numismatist*, March 1920

[4] *Annual Report of the Director of the Mint for Fiscal Year 1922*

[5] *The Numismatist*, December 1927

[6] *The Numismatist*, February 1927

[7] *The Numismatist*, July 1944

[8] *The Numismatist*, August 1932

[9] *The Numismatist*, November 1935

[10] *Rare Coin Review*, May-June 1997

[11] Breen, *Walter Breen's Complete Encyclopedia of U.S. and Colonial Coins*

[12] ibid

[13] *The Numismatic Scrapbook Magazine*, December 1943

[14] *The Numismatic Scrapbook Magazine*, July 1938

[15] *The Numismatic Scrapbook Magazine*, April 1938

[16] *The Numismatic Scrapbook Magazine*, September 1938

[17] *The Numismatic Scrapbook Magazine*, May 1938

CHAPTER 7

Proof Coinage

❧

Specimen Coinage

Proof Coinage

Proof coins of the Indian Head/Buffalo Nickel type were struck for sale to collectors from 1913 through 1916 and again in 1936 and 1937. In addition to these dates offered for public sale, proof examples are also reported with the date 1917.

The proof five-cent pieces of 1913-16 are commonly known as "matte" proofs, but this terminology is misleading. True matte proofs have a somewhat dull finish completely unlike the surfaces of normal circulation strikes, and this technique of proofing was used by the United States Mint exclusively for its gold pieces of 1908 and 1911-15, as well as for some isolated issues of later years that were not sold publicly. The technique of producing matte proofs was in vogue among medallists at the turn of the century and has been favored for that medium ever since. The slight granularity of the matte proof reinforces each design detail and is most effective when employed in high relief, fine art medals. In the lower relief typical of coinage this practice often disappoints.

The proof nickels of 1913-16, like the cents of those years, actually possess a satin finish. This varies in texture ever so slightly from one date to the next and even within a single year's coinage. When found pristine, these coins are extremely beautiful and visibly distinctive from currency strikes, no matter how well struck the latter may be. Far more common, however, are proofs that are dulled from toning or have been cleaned to remove such toning. These are the coins that create problems for collectors and dealers attempting to distinguish a proof from an ordinary coin.

The series of satin proofs issued by the United States Mint seem to be unique in that I haven't found anything comparable from the world's other mints. While this finish is distinctive to a trained eye, it's not surprising that so many people are puzzled by exactly what makes these coins proofs. So it was with collectors at the time these pieces were being offered. They longed for the striking contrast between brilliant fields and frosted relief that typified our nation's proof coinage during the 19th Century. The previous type of five-cent piece had been issued in this fashion, but the textured fields and sharply basined dies of Fraser's nickel made this brilliant style of proofing impractical.

In the May 1913 issue of *The Numismatist*, Editor Edgar H. Adams addressed collectors' frustrations regarding the proof cents and nickels:

> Proof coins have as a rule been ready for distribution to those ordering them on January 15 of each year. This year, however, because of the change in the design of the nickel, there has been a delay of about two months in getting out the minor proofs. They are at last being received by collectors. The proof of the 5-cent piece is even more unsatisfactory than that of the Lincoln cent. While the lines of the design are finer and struck up more clearly—the wrinkles on the buffalo's skin, and parts of the Indian's head, for example—the appearance of the coin is practically the same as that of the one struck for circulation. The surface of the small field is as rough, and the date and letters as liable to wear. There is the same crowding of the letters in the motto, "E Pluribus Unum," particularly in "Pluribus," where the "I" is wedged in so tightly between the "R" and the "B" as to be difficult of detection even through a very strong magnifying glass. Although a different die is supposed to have been used in striking these proofs, there is no detectable difference in design between it and that used for the nickels distributed for circulation.

However sharply defined the proofs of 1913-16 may have been, their lack of the traditional finish cut deeply into sales. Mintages declined steadily, and proof examples were not offered to collectors after 1916. Over the years a few of these proofs were spent, either by accident or in outright contempt.

The issue of what to do, if anything, about proof coinage was still pending when America entered World War I in 1917. Record production taxed the three mints to their full capacity, and there was no prospect of striking labor-intensive proof issues under such circumstances. When the war ended, the demand for additional circulating coins dropped to a trickle, but the mints were still kept busy striking medals for veterans, as well as unneeded silver dollars to fulfill the terms of the 1918 Pittman Act. The issue of proof coins was revived only occasionally during the 1920s, but the very restrictive budgets of those years didn't allow for any frills. It was not until the governmental expansion of the Roosevelt administration that money was allotted to produce proof coins.

When the sale of proofs resumed in 1936 the brilliant style was restored, but without the frosted relief that had made early proofs so stunning. The textured fields evident in Fraser's original models and in the Type 1 coinage of 1913 had been smoothed out by Barber that same year when he prepared the Type 2 reverse. This made both obverse and reverse receptive to high polishing, though such polishing also led to certain low-relief features of the dies being easily obliterated. Nevertheless, collectors were more enthusiastic about the end product. Regrettably, almost as soon as proof coinage resumed, the Buffalo Nickel was discontinued in favor of the new Jefferson type. This left only the issues of 1936 and 1937 available to collectors desiring brilliant proofs of this beautiful design.

The matte proof nickels of 1913-16 were usually sold as part of the so-called "silver proof set." This set included the cent and the nickel, in addition to the three silver pieces. It was priced at $1.16, postage additional if ordered by mail. Another option was the "minor proof set," consisting of the cent and nickel alone. This cost all of 15 cents. These options account for the fact that proof mintages for each year are not the same from one denomination to another.

The coins were presented to their purchasers in folded tissues. These tissues are the bane of today's collectors, as their high sulfur content caused the coins stored in them to develop irregular and unattractive toning. Later attempts to remove this toning often led to results even less aesthetically pleasing. The nicest surviving proofs are those removed from their wrappers at the time of purchase and stored in a less harmful environment. In a time before coin albums, this usually meant felt-lined trays stored within wooden cabinets.

The proof nickels of 1936 and 1937 were, like other denominations, sold individually. The cost of a proof Buffalo Nickel from the Philadelphia Mint was 20 cents, plus 8 cents for postage.[1] These were delivered in cellophane bags, folded and stapled at their open end. The toning effects that could result from such storage were still unpredictable, but their progress was usually much slower. Nice, original proof nickels of 1936-37 are more readily available than those of 1913-16.

Proof Date Analysis

GUIDE TO USING THIS ANALYSIS:

1. "Ranking" refers to the placement of that particular proof issue's mintage or certified population within the overall series from lowest to highest. In other words, the proof issue with the lowest mintage is 1/7, while the issue with the highest mintage is 7/7. The date having the lowest certified population appears as 1/7, and that having the highest population is ranked 7/7.

2. "TOTAL PCGS/NGC" refers to the total number of proof coins listed in the *PCGS Population Report* and the *NGC Census Report* for January 2000.

3. "VALUES" listed under 1940 are taken from the *Standard Catalogue of United States Coins and Tokens 1940*, Wayte Raymond, Editor.

4. "VALUES" listed under 1950, 1960, 1970, 1980, 1990 and 2000 are from the 4th, 13th, 23rd, 33rd, 43rd and 53rd editions of *A Guide Book of United States Coins* by R. S. Yeoman.

1913
Type 1 - Proof

Mintage:
1,520
(Ranking 5/7)

Rarity: As the first examples of their type, these proofs were ordered in large numbers. Their survival rate is a bit lower than for later issues, since these coins looked so much like regular pieces to the untrained eye than a number were probably spent. Others may lie unattributed as proofs in old collections. Gems are elusive, as these were not very appealing coins as made.

TOTAL PCGS/NGC = 433 (Ranking 3/8)

Values:		1940	1950	1960	1970	1980	1990	2000
	PR60	2.00	6.50	17.50	215.00	500.00	——	——
	PR63	——	——	——	——	——	2000	1000

Comments: If someone has not had the opportunity to examine Type 1 proofs, these may easily be confused with very well struck currency pieces. The principal difference is that the proofs have a finely-grained satin finish quite unlike the frosty brilliance typical of uncirculated regular issues. Another distinction, as always with proofs, is the extreme fullness of the borders and the sharpness of both inner and outer rims. This can be achieved only through striking a coin twice, a practice unique to proof coinage.

Another diagnostic feature of proofs is the absence of die polishing striations and erosion lines. The preparation of proof dies was performed carefully enough to preclude the former, while the latter would appear only after extended die use. Thus, it is not likely to occur with mintages in the hundreds or low thousands. The absence of these flaws does not guarantee that a coin is a proof, but their presence makes a proof attribution suspect.

The Type 1 proofs were not quite as well made as subsequent issues, perhaps due to the mint's unfamiliarity with this new coin. Of all the 1913-16 proofs, these are the most difficult to distinguish from regular coins. Authentication of a coin's proof status should be a high priority for anyone contemplating a purchase. Acquiring one already certified is the surest safeguard.

Strange as it seems, I've seen a genuine proof that had a tiny rim cud above and between the second S in STATES and the O in OF. Such flaws on proof coins are extremely rare.

1913
Type 2 - Proof

Mintage:
1,514 (Ranking 4/7)

Rarity: As the certified population suggests, this date is second only to 1916 in rarity among the early period proofs. It's almost a certainty that many of the proofs struck remained unsold at the end of the year and were melted. Those that survive are not especially attractive, particularly when compared to the proofs of 1914-16.

TOTAL PCGS/NGC = 382 (Ranking 2/8)

Values:

	1940	1950	1960	1970	1980	1990	2000
PR60	2.00	6.00	17.50	265.00	425.00	——	——
PR63	——	——	——	——	——	1300	800.00

Comments: This issue is similar in overall appearance to the Type 1 pieces, though of somewhat superior workmanship. Proofs are thus more easily distinguished from currency pieces. The advent of experienced, third-party grading services has greatly reduced the population of would-be proofs, but authentication is still recommended for those buyers not familiar with the characteristics of true proofs.

Although scarcer than the Type 1 proof, this issue is not under the same price pressure from type collectors, and this holds its value down somewhat. It is therefore consistently overlooked and probably offers a good opportunity for some bargain hunting.

1914
Proof

Mintage:
1,275 (Ranking 3/7)

Rarity: Among the 1913-16 proofs, this date is the one most often encountered, though 1913 Type 1 probably exists in greater overall numbers. The 1914 proof nickels were extremely well made, and they have a fairly high survival rate in top grades.

TOTAL PCGS/NGC = 603 (Ranking 5/8)

Values:

	1940	1950	1960	1970	1980	1990	2000
PR60	2.50	6.50	17.50	240.00	400.00	——	——
PR63	——	——	——	——	——	1200.00	700.00

Comments: The Philadelphia Mint finally polished its technique for producing proof nickels starting with this issue. The proofs of 1914-16 are of far more consistent quality than the 1913 pieces. The texture of these coins is of an even finer grain, giving them a particularly pleasing satin finish. Except in the case of toned pieces, this surface is revealed to be fairly bright, discounting the notion of these being "matte" proofs. In addition, the 1914-16 proofs have uniformly broad and complete borders, while the 1913 pieces will sometimes possess brief interruptions in the fullness of their borders.

Two features that have been cited as evidence of proof status on Type 2 Buffalo Nickels include a fine die line on the reverse border from 7 to 9 o'clock. Also noted is a triangular defect to the right of letter E in UNITED. These features are not diagnostic of proofs, rather they can appear on any boldly struck Buffalo Nickel. They were thus features of the master hub. Their appearance primarily on proofs simply reflects the more consistently sharp impressions of proof coins.

1915
Proof

Mintage:
1,050
(Ranking 2/7)

Rarity: This date is slightly scarcer than the 1914 issue, and it's likely that some portion of the 1915 mintage remained on hand the following year and was melted. Like the 1914 proofs, survivors are usually found in fairly high grades. The coins of both years were made with great care, and they seem to have retained their attractiveness despite the passing of generations.

TOTAL PCGS/NGC = 490 (Ranking 4/8)

Values:		1940	1950	1960	1970	1980	1990	2000
	PR60	2.50	7.50	18.50	265.00	400.00	——	——
	PR63	——	——	——	——	——	1500.00	900.00

Comments: The proofs of 1915 are near clones of those dated 1914. Both issues have uniformly bold strikes and satiny surfaces, though the latter quality is sometimes impaired through toning or injudicious cleaning.

Walter Breen reported that 1915 proofs are usually seen with an arcing die crack on the bison's shoulder and chest. I've seen this only rarely, and its presence is no absolute guarantee of proof status. It's believed that proof dies were used to produce regular issues once their elite service had ended, and this feature may yet turn up on a currency strike.

1916
Proof

Mintage:
600
(Ranking 1/7)

Rarity: Not surprisingly, given their low mintage, the 1916 proofs are the rarest of the early period proof Buffalo Nickels. Some portion of the 600 pieces coined was almost certainly consigned to oblivion when the Mint ceased sales of proof coins at the end of this year. Among the rare survivors, gems are the rule. It seems that collectors recognized the added value of these proofs early on and took care to preserve them.

TOTAL PCGS/NGC = 306 (Ranking 1/8)

Values:

	1940	1950	1960	1970	1980	1990	2000
PR60	5.00	10.00	35.00	395.00	500.00	——	——
PR63	——	——	——	——	——	2500	1400

Comments: As with the currency strikes, all proof dies for 1916 were sunk from the new obverse hub featuring a much bolder LIBERTY.

The surfaces of these proofs reveal the finely-grained satin finish used for 1914 and 1915, but the 1916 nickels are even brighter and remarkably beautiful. In combination with the sharpened design of the new obverse hub, the proof nickels of 1916 represent the very pinnacle of quality for this coin type. Unfortunately, the 1916 proofs are also far scarcer and quite a bit more expensive than the proofs of 1913-15.

In addition to having a small mintage, it's possible that unsold pieces may have been destroyed at the Mint. Whether or not all 600 pieces were actually distributed thus remains unknown. Because they were not sufficiently distinctive from regular coins, matte and satin proofs had fallen out of favor with most collectors, though there were those speculators who made a practice of buying any unsold proofs at the end of each year.

Traditionally, proof coins were made available for sale in January, suggesting that they may have been the very first coins struck at the Philadelphia Mint each year. Collectors had come to count on this fact and were dismayed when the delivery of proof coins for 1915 and 1916 was held up without explanation. While the Mint awaited the new models for the dime, quarter dollar and half dollar, it was reluctant to produce any silver pieces of the old types. Delays in adoption of the new models eventually forced production of Barber Dimes and Quarters beginning in the summer, but the Mint still declined to strike proofs of these pieces dated 1916. Ultimately, the only proof coins made for sale in 1916 were the cent and five-cent piece.

Frustration with this new development led the American Numismatic Association to pass a resolution addressing the matter during its 1916 convention in Baltimore.[2] Its efforts were in vain, however, as no proof specimens of the silver and gold coins were made available. A few examples of the new silver designs were coined in proof, but these went to privileged parties.

The sale of proof coins of any denomination was suspended after 1916. This was due both to disappointment with the existing style of proofs and a realization that the newly adopted silver types would be even more difficult to coin in proof.

1917
Proof (?)

Mintage:
Unknown

TOTAL PR PCGS/NGC = 0

(Photos courtesy Norm Talbert)

Comments: At least one and possibly two 1917 nickels have had proof status conferred upon them by the late Walter Breen. These exhibit a pronounced wire rim on the obverse from 7 to 10 o'clock and on the reverse from 1 to 5 o'clock. While this is typical of coins struck twice or from very closely set dies, it is not a feature seen on the proof nickels of 1913-16.

No proof nickels were reported or offered to the public in 1917, yet Breen allegedly authenticated as many as seven! I've had the opportunity to see only one, the piece illustrated above. I examined it carefully when it was submitted to NGC for certification as a proof. While it did exhibit an extremely strong strike from unworn dies, it simply did not possess the characteristics of the 1913-16 proofs. Its surfaces were of a slightly different texture, and it simply lacked the overall "look" of a proof, knowledge of which only experience can impart. I agreed with NGC's grading team that it did not merit proof status.

This has been the fate of any 1917 coins submitted to the major grading services as proofs. To date, not one 1917 coin of any denomination has been certified and encapsulated as a proof. Until this happens, the purported proofs of this date will enjoy only a shadowy existence.

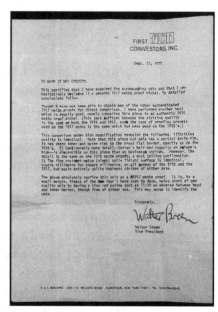

Walter Breen's authentication
of the example illustrated
(Talbert)

1936
Proof

Mintage:
4,420
(Ranking 6/7)

Rarity: Though both the mintage and survival rate of this date greatly exceed those of all previous Buffalo Nickel proofs, the demand for 1936 proofs, particularly in the brilliant finish, is tremendous. This issue is significantly scarcer than the 1937 proofs, however, and gems are in the minority. For more information regarding the rarity of satin versus brilliant proofs, see Comments below.

TOTAL SATIN PCGS/NGC = 864 (Ranking 7/8)

TOTAL BRILLIANT PCGS/NGC = 847 (Ranking 6/8)

Values:

	1940	1950	1960	1970	1980	1990	2000
PR60	1.50	10.00	120.00	150.00	700.00	——	——
PR63	——	——	——	——	——	1650.00	——
PR65	——	——	——	——	——	——	900.00

Comments: On April 28, 1936 Treasury Secretary Henry Morgenthau authorized the Mint to resume selling proof coins to collectors. This developed from a suggestion reportedly made to President Franklin Roosevelt by his secretary, Louis McHenry Howe.[3]

The 1936 proof coins of all denominations varied slightly in their overall finish. This quality was obvious only on the cents and nickels, perhaps due to the lesser reflectivity of their metals. 1936 proofs of either style feature sharp high-point details, distinct inner and outer rims, and broader than usual borders.

The first coins sold possessed a satin finish that Breen described as "sometimes almost matte." These accounted for approximately two-thirds of the total proof mintage, though their surviving population is less than that of the later, more brilliant coins. In his 1988 encyclopedia, Breen quoted 1960s dealer Lester Merkin as stating that the satin proofs were five times as rare as the brilliant proofs, but the advent of certified grading has revealed that there is little distinction in available numbers. Breen attributed the alleged rarity of satin proofs to the poor reception given them by collectors, many of whom may ultimately spent the coins either by accident or in outright contempt. He even reported having found examples of both types in circulation during the late 1940s and early 1950s, though Walter was known to spin some good yarns.

When the Mint's employees had finally mastered the art of coining proofs, the pieces that resulted were of a fully brilliant finish, as on later proof coins through the 1960s. These were far more popular, and their survival rate is somewhat higher than for the satin proofs. Even so, the greater popularity of the brilliant proofs continues to this day and accounts for the premium that they enjoy over their scarcer brothers.

Unless they've been dipped, most 1936 proof nickels show some degree of toning. This usually takes the form of a hazy or milky film on both sides. Not especially attractive, it is still valued as a mark of "originality."

Beware of alterations made to regular 1936 nickels in an attempt to pass them as proofs. Many pieces have been buffed or plated with either chromium or mercury to simulate proof coins. These are readily detected by experienced numismatists, such as those at third-party grading services. Simulated proofs will typically lack the fullness of strike seen on real proofs. The knot of the Indian's hair braid is usually the last part of the die to fill, and this is a good diagnostic point for proofs.

1937
Proof

Mintage:
5,769
(Ranking 7/7)

Rarity: While its mintage is miniscule by the standards of recent decades, this is the most readily available of proof Buffalo Nickels. Though a number of pieces have been impaired, even gems turn up with some frequency.

TOTAL PCGS/NGC = 2355 (Ranking 7/7)

Values:

	1940	1950	1960	1970	1980	1990	2000
PR60	.85	5.50	50.00	85.00	650.00	——	——
PR63	——	——	——	——	——	1200.00	——
PR65	——	——	——	——	——	——	800.00

Comments: All proofs of this date have fully brilliant fields, devices and edges. This is the most readily obtainable proof Buffalo Nickel, and it is often available in gem condition. Some have hazy toning that may or may not be attractive. A rare minority will show delightful, multicolor toning from long-term storage in coin albums. As with all brilliant proofs, look carefully for the tiny hairline scratches that can be so detrimental to a proof coin's grade and value.

Though fully struck, these proofs still lack the fine detail of the 1913-16 proofs. Some of the subtler lines had simply worn away from the master hubs after the large regular mintages of 1916-20 forced the production of so many dies.

As with 1936 proofs, beware of well struck currency pieces that have been polished to simulate proof brilliance. These will be lacking the high point detail and broad, flat rims typical of proofs. The widespread use of third-party certification services has largely eliminated this evil, but caution is still advised when purchasing uncertified or "raw" proofs.

To see just how deceptive a sharply struck circulation strike can be, compare the above proof to the 1937-P nickel illustrated in the date and mint analysis for regular issues (see Chapter 6). The latter is every bit as sharp as the proof in its central details, but the illusion is dispelled when one looks at the leftmost feather. Note how flat the tip is on the regular coin. This would never be seen on a true proof, which by definition must exhibit a virtually perfect strike.

The numismatic community was surprised in 1989 with the announcement that three 1927-P nickels had been certified as "specimen" strikings by Numismatic Guaranty Corporation. Since that time, two additional examples of this remarkable issue have surfaced, and these have likewise been certified by NGC.

Nearly everyone who viewed these coins agreed that they were something special. What their exact nature is remains something of a mystery. They are known to possess the following distinguishing features: extremely sharp details, squared lettering and borders, wire rims and a satiny obverse and reverse with reflective edges. All of these are characteristic of proof coins, and indeed the 1927 "specimen" nickels have been compared in appearance to the satin finish proofs of 1936.

After studying one of the first three pieces discovered, Walter Breen penned the following letter that was published in *Coin World*:[4]

> This certifies that I have examined the accompanying coin and that I unhesitatingly declare it a genuine 1927 Satin Finish Proof Buffalo nickel.
>
> Compared to Uncirculated business strikes of 1927, the present coin is overwhelmingly superior: sharper in all relief details (hair, feathers, bison's hide), with "squared" inner rims, broad flat rims with complete knife rims, in all details comparable to 1913-16 and 1936 "Type I" Proofs. Surfaces are satin finish and untampered. (The diagonal line on reverse flat rim about 8 o'clock is in the original die from which hubs and working dies came; no business strikes are brought up enough in strike to show it.)
>
> All features point to at least two perfectly aligned blows from the dies, as normal in Proofs but not business strikes. Surfaces are like those of "Roman finish" 1909-10 gold Proofs, and certain Proof commemoratives.
>
> To call this coin unprecedented is rea-

1927 "Specimen" Nickel
(Larry Whitlow)

sonable; to call it extraordinary is an understatement.

Speculation as to why and how such coins were made has led to several theories. The first of these relates to the Mint's Chief Engraver from 1925 to 1947, John R. Sinnock. He was known to have had a taste for matte or satin proofs, as he had examples struck for his own collection on several occasions. Generally, such clandestine coining was limited to new designs, the commemorative half dollar series being a particular favorite of his. Several unofficial proof coins turned up in his estate when it was auctioned in 1962. No mention was made in the catalog of specimen or proof nickels dated 1927, yet there were several examples of this date included in group lots with other Buffalo Nickels. Again, no special status was attached to these coins, but it is believed that among those unassuming nickels were to be found the five or more "specimen" strikings now known.

Another possible explanation that has been offered is that these coins were struck for presentation to the members of the Annual Assay Commission. The time-honored custom of assembling government officials and distinguished members of the general public to test the standards of the nation's coinage was performed early in each calendar year until suspended by President Carter in 1977. The public members of the commission each received a specially prepared medal for their participation, this medal marking the occasion and year of their service.

There is no documentation of actual coins ever being distributed to commission members, and it seems likely that if such a step were undertaken the humble five-cent piece would hardly be a fitting souvenir, handsome though it may be. A silver dollar or gold piece would be more likely used for this purpose. All things considered, this particular explanation for the existence of proof or specimen nickels dated 1927 does not merit much consideration.

The most intriguing theory put forth is that these coins were actually test pieces that resulted from the Mint's experiments with chromium-plated dies and collars. *The Annual Report of the Director of the Mint* for fiscal years 1928 and 1929 reveal that the Philadelphia Mint began such experiments when commissioned to produce coinage for the nation of Ecuador. Being of pure nickel, these coins were more destructive to dies and machinery than the alloys previously employed. The 1929 report states that while the chromium plating was successful in completing the Ecuadoran coinage, the average life of a die was less than when coining copper-nickel. This may be read as suggesting that at least some coinage occurred with chromium plated dies using copper-nickel planchets, otherwise there could be no valid comparison made. Since the United States five-cent piece is routinely struck in copper-nickel, might such coins have been the test-bed for chromium plating?

The nickel coins struck for Ecuador are dated 1928. The inclusion of chromium plating experiments in the 1928 report, which covers the period from July 1, 1927 through June 30, 1928, suggests that the Ecuadoran coinage was performed early in the year. It is therefore possible that the initial experiments may have been performed using regular United States coin dies dated 1927. Whether or not this accounts for the 1927 specimen nickels is uncertain, as no specific documentation exists to support this speculation.

Mark Van Winkle studied the matter closely and may have found evidence that links the use of chromium plated dies to these special strikings. He presented his findings in a numismatic theater presentation at the Seattle convention of the American Numismatic Association in 1990. In addition to the above references found within the Mint Director's reports, a close examination of the surfaces of one of the 1927 specimen nick-

Micro-cracking in the reverse die
(Mark Van Winkle)

Micro-cracking; the heavy diagonal lines between the bison's legs are die polishing lines
(Van Winkle)

Micro-cracking in the reverse die
(Van Winkle)

Micro-cracking in the reverse die
(Van Winkle)

Micro-cracking in the reverse die
(Van Winkle)

els revealed the presence of a phenomenon known as "micro-cracking."

In conversations with George Hunter, the U. S. Mint's director of technology, Van Winkle learned that chromium plating has been used routinely for the preparation of proof dies since 1972. In addition to extending the useful life of a proof die, one by-product of this practice is the appearance of micro-cracking. This is described as a "crazing pattern" or "dry river bed look" in the fields of a coin. Of course, for it to be present on the coin it must have been present on the die, as well. The prevalence of micro-cracking is greatest toward the edge of the coin, and it cannot be seen without magnification. Although it occurs routinely with proof coins stuck from chromium plated dies, it is not known for currency strikes. In fact, its only other appearance thus far noted has been on the 1927 specimen nickels.

By combining two of the above theories a possible explanation may be found for these unusual coins. If it is supposed that experiments were conducted with copper-nickel planchets using chromium plated Buffalo Nickels dies, wouldn't these coins have made a nice addition to Chief Engraver Sinnock's collection of private rarities? This notion is not at all far-fetched. The proof commemorative coins that turned up in Sinnock's estate were once unimaginable but are now readily accepted as fact. If these nickels have not fully been accepted as genuine proofs, perhaps they now should be.

Before leaving the subject of specimen coins, some mention must be made of the alleged specimen pieces dated 1919 and 1935. Single examples of each date have been reported, though neither has been so certified. Walter Breen examined the 1935 specimen at the 1989 Pittsburgh A.N.A. convention and wrote the following letter, which is provided courtesy of Tom Arch:

> This certifies that I have examined the accompanying coin and that I unhesitatingly declare it genuine as described below.
>
> It is a 1935 Buffalo nickel described as a "specimen striking." It has extraordinary sharpness, obviously and visibly from two blows of the dies. This extra impression has imparted not only extra design detail as on proofs but extra sharpness on inner and outer rims, again as on proofs. Surfaces are satiny, though unlike either the 1916, 1917, 1927 or 1936 Type I proofs; it is uncertain if any special treatment was done to the surfaces as normally with proofs.
>
> This is the first such piece I have seen.

Though Breen seems to have been convinced of this coin's special status, I've not had the opportunity to examine it firsthand. No further information has come to my attention regarding the 1919 and 1935 specimen strikings.

Footnotes to Chapter 7

[1] *The Numismatic Scrapbook Magazine,* May 1936
[2] *The Numismatist,* October 1916
[3] *The Numismatic Scrapbook Magazine,* May 1936
[4] Giedroyc, Richard. "Breen declares Indian Head 5-cent coin a Proof"

APPENDICES

Glossary

❧

Statistics

❧

Bibliography

Glossary

ANAAB – American Numismatic Association Authentication Bureau. It is owned and operated by the American Numismatic Association and maintains files on counterfeit and altered coins. It also renders opinions as to the authenticity of coins and performs conservation services for coins.

ANACS – Formerly owned by the American Numismatic Association and now under commercial ownership, it authenticates, grades and encapsulates coins.

BASINING – Describes the process of preparing a working die for placement into the press. The die face is held against rotating grinding surfaces angled at various degrees to impart the proper contour or die face radii. Successful basining allows for a smooth flow of metal into all recesses of the die during coining. This preparation is made at the mint of use, rather than being limited to the Philadelphia Mint where dies are initially created. As a result, coins struck at different mints will often possess a unique character that identifies their origin nearly as well as the mintmark does.

BROADSTRIKE – A coin struck outside of the restraining collar. Broadstrikes are oversize in diameter and may show a partial collar strike, known as a "railroad rim" (see Chapter 3).

CURRENCY STRIKE – A regular production coin, struck only once and intended for use in commerce. The term "business strike" is also used.

COLLAR – The steel ring that surrounds the coining chamber between obverse and reverse dies. Modern coins are struck within a "close" collar in which the expanding edge of the planchet is forcefully restrained against the collar's inner surface. Buffalo Nickels were coined within a "plain," close collar, and they have no design on their edge.

CUD – A coin variety in which a portion of the die has broken away, usually as the result of a progressive die crack. This missing portion appears as a blank or filled-in area on the coin and is known colloquially as a cud. The correct numismatic term is "major die break."

DDO – Doubled-die obverse. When a working die is not accurately in register between multiple impressions from a working hub, a slight doubling or shifting of the image is imparted to the die. This doubling then appears on all coins struck from that die.

DDR – Doubled die reverse. See above for explanation.

DIE – A steel cylinder that bears on one end a negative or incuse image of a coin design. Master dies are used to raise working hubs, while working dies are used to strike coins. In striking Buffalo Nickels, the reverse die was used as the upper or "hammer" die, while the obverse was positioned as the lower or "anvil" die.

HUB – A steel cylinder which bears on one end a positive or relief image of a coin design. A master hub is used to sink master dies, while working hubs are used to sink working dies.

MECHANICAL OR STRIKE DOUBLING – This occurs when one or both dies move laterally or rotate slightly at the moment of striking. The result is a shallow doubled image on devices and/or lettering. This kind of doubling is flat and shelf-like, rather than showing the contoured doubling typical of a doubled-die variety. Such coins are not considered varieties and have no added value.

NGC – Numismatic Guaranty Corporation of America. A commercial service that authenticates, grades and encapsulates coins. The quantities of certified Buffalo Nickels used in this book were taken from the *NGC Census Report* for January 2000.

OMM – Overmintmark variety, an example being D over S (abbreviated as D/S).

ORIGINAL ROLL – Coins are delivered to the Federal Reserve Banks from the mint in bags or boxes, never in rolls. Thus, uncirculated rolls are wrapped by banks from freshly delivered coins. "Original" rolls consist of coins that have been kept together since new and have not been picked through by collectors who then substituted lesser coins for the finer pieces.

PCGS – Professional Coin Grading Service is a commercial service that authenticates, grades and encapsulates coins. The quantities of certified Buffalo Nickels used in this book were taken from the *PCGS Population Report* for January 2000.

PROOF – A coin made from specially polished dies and planchets and struck two or more times to bring out all details. These are intended for presentation as gifts or for sale to collectors at a premium (see Chapter 7).

RANKING – The sequence by quantity made from lowest to highest for each date. For example, out of seven dates of proof nickels sold to the public, 1916 has the lowest mintage at 600 pieces. Therefore, its ranking is (1/7).

RARITY RATING – The relative rarity of a particular date with respect to others in the series (see Chapter 5).

RPM – Repunched mintmark variety, an example being D over D (abbreviated as D/D).

SLIDER – Refers to a coin that appears uncirculated and may be offered as such but which possesses the very slightest wear. The corresponding numerical grade is AU58.

TWO-FEATHERS – A variety in which the shallow, innermost feather on the Indian's portrait has been obliterated by polishing of the die.

Statistics

TABLE 1. *The ranking of Buffalo Nickels by mintage from lowest to highest.*

RANK	DATE	MINTAGE	RANK	DATE	MINTAGE
1	1926-S	970,000	33	1920-D	9,418,000
2	1931-S	1,200,000	34	1920-S	9,689,000
3	1913-S T2	1,209,000	35	1917-D	9,910,000
4	1924-S	1,437,000	36	1935-S	10,300,000
5	1915-S	1,505,000	37	1921	10,663,000
6	1921-S	1,557,000	38	1916-S	11,860,000
7	1913-S T1	2,105,000	39	1935-D	12,092,000
8	1927-S	3,430.000	40	1916-D	13,333,000
9	1914-S	3,470,000	41	1936-S	14,930,000
10	1914-D	3,912,000	42	1937-D	17,826,000
11	1913-D T2	4,156,000	43	1934	20,213,003
12	1917-S	4,193,000	44	1914	20,665,738
13	1925-D	4,450,000	45	1915	20,987,270
14	1918-S	4,882,000	46	1924	21,620,000
15	1924-D	5,258,000	47	1930	22,849,000
16	1913-D T1	5,337,000	48	1928	23,411,000
17	1930-S	5,435,000	49	1936-D	24,814,000
18	1937-S	5,635,000	50	1913 T2	29,858,700
19	1926-D	5,638,000	51	1913 T1	30,993,520
20	1927-D	5,730,000	52	1918	32,086,314
21	1923-S	6,142,000	53	1925	35,565,100
22	1925-S	6,256,000	54	1923	35,715,000
23	1928-D	6,436,000	55	1929	36,446,000
24	1928-S	6,936,000	56	1927	37,981,000
25	1938-D	7,020,000	57	1926	44,693,000
26	1934-D	7,480,000	58	1917	51,424,019
27	1919-S	7,521,000	59	1935	58,264,000
28	1915-D	7,569,000	60	1919	60,868,000
29	1929-S	7,754,000	61	1920	63,093,000
30	1919-D	8,006,000	62	1916	63,498,066
31	1918-D	8,362,000	63	1937	79,485,769
32	1929-D	8,370,000	64	1936	119,001,420

TABLE 2. *Rarity Ratings by Grade for Buffalo Nickels (See page 68 for definitions of Rarity Ratings.)*

Grades G-VG

R4	1913-S T2				
R3	1913-S T1	1913-D T2	1914-D	1914-S	1917-S	1931-S
R2	1913 T1	1913-D T1	1913 T2	1914	1915	1915-D
	1915-S	1916-D	1916-S	1917-D	1918	1918-D
	1918-S	1919-D	1919-S	1920-D	1921-S	1924
	1924-D	1924-S	1925-D	1926-D	1926-S	1927-D
	1938-D					
R1	1916	1917	1919	1920	1920-S	1921
	1923	1923-S	1925	1925-S	1926	1927
	1927-S	1928	1928-D	1928-S	1929	1929-D
	1929-S	1930	1930-S	1934	1934-D	1935
	1935-D	1935-S	1936	1936-D	1936-S	1937
	1937-D	1937-S				

Grade Fine

R4	1913-S T2	1917-S			
R3	1913-S T1	1913-D T2	1914-D	1915-D	1915-S	1918
	1918-D	1920-D	1921-S	1924-S	1925-D	1926-S
R2	1913-P T1	1913-D T1	1913 T2	1914	1914-S	1915
	1916-D	1916-S	1917-D	1918-S	1919-D	1919-S
	1920-S	1921	1923-S	1924	1924-D	1925-S
	1926-D	1927-D	1927-S	1928-D	1929-D	1931-S
	1938-D					
R1	1916	1917	1919	1920	1923	1925
	1926	1927	1928	1928-S	1929	1929-S
	1930	1930-S	1934	1934-D	1935	1935-D
	1935-S	1936	1936-D	1936-S	1937	1937-D
	1937-S					

Grade VF

R5	1924-S				
R4	1915-S	1917-S	1920-D	1921-S	1925-D	
R3	1913-D T2	1913-S T2	1914-D	1917-D	1918	1918-D
	1918-S	1919-D	1919-S	1920-S	1921	1923-S
	1924-D	1925-S	1926-D	1926-S	1927-D	1927-S
	1928-D					
R2	1913 T1	1913-D T1	1913-S T1	1913 T2	1914	1914-S
	1915	1915-D	1916	1916-D	1916-S	1917
	1919	1920	1923	1924	1925	1926
	1927	1928	1928-S	1929	1929-D	1930-S
	1931-S	1934-D	1935-D			
R1	1929-S	1930	1934	1935	1935-S	1936
	1936-D	1936-S	1937	1937-D	1937-S	1938-D

Grades XF-AU

R5	1921-S	1924-S	1925-D			
R4	1915-S	1917-D	1917-S	1918	1918-D	1918-S
	1919-D	1919-S	1920-D	1924-D	1925-S	1926-S
	1927-D	1928-D				
R3	1913-D T2	1913-S T2	1914-D	1915-D	1920-S	1921
	1923-S	1924	1926-D	1927-S	1928-S	1929-D
	1934-D	1935-D				

R2	1913-D T1	1913-S T1	1913 T2	1914	1914-S	1915
	1916	1916-D	1916-S	1917	1919	1920
	1923	1925	1926	1927	1928	1929
	1929-S	1930	1930-S	1931-S	1934	1935-S
R1	1913 T1	1935	1936	1936-D	1936-S	1937
	1937-D	1937-S	1938-D			

Grades MS60-63

R5	1926-S					
R4	1913-S T2	1918-S	1919-D	1919-S	1920-D	1920-S
	1921-S	1924-S	1925-D	1925-S	1927-S	
R3	1913-D T2	1914-D	1915-D	1915-S	1916-S	1917-D
	1917-S	1918	1918-D	1921	1923-S	1924
	1924-D	1928-S	1929-D			
R2	1913-D T1	1913-S T1	1913 T2	1914	1914-S	1915
	1916	1916-D	1917	1919	1920	1923
	1925	1926	1926-D	1927	1927-D	1928
	1928-D	1929	1929-S	1930	1930-S	1931-S
	1934	1934-D	1935-D			
R1	1913-P T1	1935	1935-S	1936	1936-D	1936-S
	1937	1937-D	1937-S	1938-D		

Grade MS64

R6	1925-S					
R5	1920-S	1926-S				
R4	1913-S T2	1918-D	1918-S	1919-D	1919-S	1920-D
	1921	1921-S	1923-S	1924-S	1925-D	1926-D
	1927-S					
R3	1913-S T1	1913 T2	1913-D T2	1914-D	1914-S	1915-D
	1915-S	1916-D	1916-S	1917-D	1917-S	1918
	1923	1924	1924-D	1927-D	1928-S	1929-D
	1934	1934-D	1935-D			
R2	1913 T1	1913-D T1	1914	1915	1916	1917
	1919	1920	1925	1926	1927	1928
	1928-D	1929	1929-S	1930	1930-S	1931-S
	1935-S					
R1	1935	1936	1936-D	1936-S	1937	1937-D
	1937-S	1938-D				

Grades MS65

R7	1920-S	1925-S	1926-S			
R6	1918-S	1923-S	1924-S	1927-S		
R5	1913-S T2	1916-D	1918-D	1919-D	1919-S	1920-D
	1921-S	1925-D	1927-D	1928-S		
R4	1913-S T1	1913 T2	1913-D T2	1914-D	1914-S	1915-D
	1915-S	1916-S	1917	1917-D	1917-S	1918
	1921	1923	1924	1924-D	1925	1926-D
	1928-D	1929-D	1934-D	1935-D		
R3	1913-D T1	1914	1915	1916	1919	1920
	1927	1928	1929	1929-S	1930	1930-S
	1934	1935-S				
R2	1913 T1	1926	1931-S	1935	1936-D	1936-S
	1937-D	1937-S				
R1	1936	1937	1938-D			

TABLE 3. *The combined quantity by date and mint of Buffalo Nickels certified as mint state by PCGS and NGC (as of January 2000) and their resulting rank from the least to the greatest number certified.*

RANK	DATE	CERTIFIED	RANK	DATE	CERTIFIED
1/2	1924-S	257	33	1917	1,037
1/2	1926-S	257	34	1916-D	1,071
3	1921-S	325	35	1925	1,076
4	1917-S	372	36	1934	1,109
5	1919-D	391	37	1928	1,155
6	1918-S	404	38	1929-S	1,189
7	1919-S	412	39	1914-S	1,198
8	1920-D	435	40	1919	1,230
9	1927-S	453	41	1914	1,378
10	1920-S	495	42	1929	1,423
11	1918-D	500	43	1927	1,434
12	1924-D	559	44	1913-S T1	1,532
13	1925-S	564	45	1935-D	1,543
14	1917-D	593	46	1934-D	1,595
15	1915-S	611	47	1915	1,603
16	1925-D	659	48	1935	1,749
17	1915-D	689	49	1930	1,858
18	1928-S	690	50	1913 T2	1,892
19	1923-S	704	51	1928-D	1,921
20	1918	706	52	1916	1,976
21	1924	710	53	1935-S	2,028
22	1913-D T2	757	54	1936-D	2,032
23	1926-D	806	55	1926	2,127
24/25	1916-S	809	56	1936-S	2,193
24/25	1927-D	809	57	1913-D T1	2,288
26	1921	817	58	1931-S	2,749
27	1914-D	826	59	1936	3,095
28	1913-S T2	838	60	1937-S	3,977
29	1929-D	924	61	1937-D	4,671
30	1930-S	927	62	1913 T1	8,769
31	1920	961	63	1937	9,560
32	1923	1,023	64	1938-D	47,028

TABLE 4. *The combined total of proof Buffalo Nickels certified by PCGS and NGC (as of January 2000), their resulting rank and the percentage of their mintage that the certified population represents.*

RANK	DATE	CERTIFIED	PERCENTAGE
1	1916	306	51.0
2	1913 T2	382	25.2
3	1913 T1	433	28.5
4	1915	490	46.7
5	1914	603	47.3
6	1936 Brilliant	847	19.2
7	1936 Satin	864	19.5
8	1937	2,355	40.8

Bibliography

BOOKS:

American Numismatic Association. *Counterfeit Detection, Volumes I & II.* ANA. Colorado Springs, CO, 1983 & 1988.

Breen, Walter. *Walter Breen's Complete Encyclopedia of U.S. and Colonial Coins.* F.C.I. Press, Inc. & Doubleday. New York, 1988.

Breen, Walter. *Walter Breen's Encyclopedia of United States and Colonial Proof Coins 1722-1977.* F.C.I. Press, Inc. Albertson, NY, 1977.

Bressett, Ken & A. Kosoff. *Official A.N.A. Grading Standards for United States Coins*, Fifth Edition. American Numismatic Association. Colorado Springs, CO, 1996.

Barsness, Larry. *The Bison in Art.* Northland Press. Fort Worth, TX, 1977.

Cohen, Annette R. & Ray M. Druley. *The Buffalo Nickel.* Potomac Enterprises. Arlington, VA, 1979.

Dary, David A. *The Buffalo Book.* The Swallow Press, Inc. Chicago, 1974.

Fivaz, Bill & J. T. Stanton; Mike Ellis, Editor. *The Cherrypickers' Guide to Rare Die Varieties*, Fourth Edition. Bowers & Merena Galleries, Inc. Wolfeboro, NH, 2000.

Judd, J. Hewitt, M.D. *United States Pattern, Experimental and Trial Pieces*, Sixth Edition. Western Publishing Co. Racine, WI, 1977.

Margolis, Arnold. *How Error Coins are Made in the U.S. Mints.* Heigh Ho Printing. Newbury Park, CA, 1981.

Morris, Joseph F. (Editor). *James Earle Fraser.* University of Georgia Press, 1955.

Rochette, Edward C. *Making Money: Rogues & Rascals Who Made Their Own.* Renaissance House. Frederick, CO, 1986.

Romines, Delma K. *Hobo Nickels.* Lonesome John Publishing Co. Newbury Park, CA, 1982.

Taxay, Don. *The U.S. Mint and Coinage.* Arco Publishing Co., Inc. New York, 1966.

United States Treasury Department. *Annual Report of the Director of the Mint for Fiscal Year Ended June 30, 1922.* U. S. Government Printing Office. Washington, DC, 1922.

United States Treasury Department. *Annual Report of the Director of the Mint for Fiscal Year Ended June 30, 1928.* U. S. Government Printing Office. Washington, DC, 1928.

United States Treasury Department. *Annual Report of the Director of the Mint for Fiscal Year Ended June 30, 1929.* U. S. Government Printing Office. Washington, DC, 1929.

United States Treasury Department. *Domestic and Foreign Coins Manufactured by Mints of the United States 1793-1980.* U. S. Government Printing Office. Washington, DC, 1981.

Vermeule, Cornelius. *Numismatic Art in America.* The Belknap Press of Harvard University Press. Cambridge, MA, 1971.

Wescott, Michael. *The United States Nickel Five-Cent Piece.* Bowers & Merena Galleries, Inc. Wolfeboro, NH, 1991.

Wexler, John A. & Tom Miller. *The RPM Book.* Lonesome John Publishing Co. Newbury Park, CA, 1983.

Wexler, John A., Ron Pope & Kevin Flynn. *Treasure Hunting Buffalo Nickels.* Stanton Publishing. Savannah, GA, 1999.

Yeoman, R. S., Kenneth Bresset (editor). *A Guide Book of United States Coins*, various editions. St. Martin's Press. New York.

PERIODICALS:

Anderson, Burnett. "Senator requests Buffalo nickel reissue in silver." *Numismatic News.* June 20, 1995.

Bowers, Q. David (editor). "A 'Gem' From R. W. Julian." *Rare Coin Review.* No. 117, May-June 1997.

Cohen, Annette R. & Ray M. Druley (editors). "Fraser Plaster Models Sold at Auction." *Buffalo Nickel Report.* January 15, 1981.

Ganz, David L. "Washington Roundup: Turnover Time at the Mint." *Coinage.* June 2000.

Giedroyc, Richard. "Breen declares Indian Head 5-cent coin a Proof." *Coin World.* June 21, 1989.

Hewitt, Lee F. "Proof Coins Authorized." *Numismatic Scrapbook.* May 1936.

Ratzman, Leonard J. "The Buffalo Nickel, A 50-Year-Old Mystery." *The Whitman Numismatic Journal.* May & June 1964.

Reed, Fred. "Lincoln Lore: Buffalo Nickel Designer Had a Penchant for Honest Abe." *Heritage Insider.* December 1999.

Sidman, Ray. "Lucas spearheads commemorative coin bill." *Numismatic News.* May 2, 2000.

Van Allen, Leroy & Marilyn. "Couple Discovers 'Five-Legged Buffalo'." *Coin World.* January 6, 1992.

Whitlow, Larry. "Buffalo Nickels: A Study of Relative Rarity in MS-65 Condition." *The Coin Dealer Newsletter Monthly Summary.* Hollywood, CA, February 1977.

AUCTION CATALOGS:

Kelly & Charlton. *The ANA/CNA Sale.* August 1962.

Mid-American Rare Coin Auctions. *The ANA Midwinter Sale.* March 1989.

Joseph Lepczyk. *Public Auction and Mail Bid Sale Number 36.* October 1980.

VIDEO:

Van Ryzin, Bob. "The Buffalo Nickel Hoax." Presented at the American Numismatic Association Numismatic Theater. Media Resource Corp., 1990.

UNPUBLISHED MATERIAL:

National Archives of the United States. Record Group 104. Files 308449, 305310 and 305927

Van Winkle, Mark. Research notes on the 1927 specimen nickels prepared for the 1990 ANA Numismatic Theater.

WHY the Coin Dealer newsletter *family of publications* remains the UNDISPUTED PRICING LEADER

The Broadest Source of Information...

Our comprehensive (and often exclusive) sources of trading information allow the **CDN** to report coin market activity in the most thorough manner possible. Our senior staff monitors **all** daily teletype buying and selling messages; we carefully evaluate sight-unseen and sight-seen Bids and Asks on all computer systems, auction results, private treaty sales between dealers (often unpublicized), and every other source of wholesale pricing information. Our dealer-to-dealer Bid & Ask

levels are thoroughly and realistically researched—giving our subscribers all of the facts needed to make informed buying and selling decisions!

The Assurance of Accuracy...

The CDN does not buy or sell coins, nor

do staff members. Here the advantage to subscribers is obvious! Since the CDN has no "position" in the market, it is able to report price changes in a frank and unbiased manner.

The Reliability of Independence...

The CDN does not use the "Panel of Experts" approach. Although our contact with dealers, big & small, is constant, we do not simply use prices submitted by any dealer or group of dealers. Logic dictates that this approach would not be in the best interest of our subscribers. 'Input' from dealers is certainly important — but must be carefully weighed against all our other sources of dealer-to-dealer trading information.

The Most Complete Market Coverage Available...

Our publications cover the *entire* coin market, not just 'selected issues'. Subscribers to the CDN receive the weekly *Coin Dealer newsletter* (the "*Greysheet*"), featuring up-to-date information on the most important and fast-moving market segments. At no extra charge, they also receive the **CDN Monthly Supplement**, providing pricing in all tradeable grades of complete series listed by date (i.e. all Barber coinage), and the **CDN Quarterly** (one section is issued every month). Every regular issue U.S. coin is accurately priced; tens of thousands of prices are updated monthly!

Subscribers to the **Certified Coin Dealer** *newsletter* (the "*Bluesheet*") receive weekly reports of the most important PCGS and NGC certified coins trading in the wholesale marketplace. Additional pricing supplements every month cover PL Morgans, Early Gold, Better Date Issues, Matte Proofs, Standing Lib Quarters, Franklin Halves, and St. Gaudens $20s. Once each month we cover selected issues certified by ANACS, PCI, INS, and NCI as well. And now, once a month, the "*Bluesheet*" also includes Ask & Trade prices; your buying and selling decisions require this information, found only in the CCDN—and all for the same low price.

Currency dealers and collectors all turn to the **Currency Dealer** *newsletter* (the "*Greensheet*") for the wholesale prices needed to actively participate in the joys of collecting paper money. Large & small sized U.S. issues are covered, in multiple grades — all the way from VG to Gem CU. This is the market's only source for dealer-to-dealer pricing information.

In-Depth Analyses & Market Comment...

All of our publications give you more than just pricing charts — we also feature market analysis through our regular columns and special guest features, charts, graphs and indices. Need a thorough examination of a certain series? We have probably covered it! Our analyses have long been hailed as the definitive studies of the areas covered.

Experience Still Counts for Everything...

The CDN has reported on coin market activity *since 1963*, and our senior staff shares *nearly a century* of professional numismatic experience. This unparalleled experience places the CDN in the unique and enviable position to accurately evaluate the enormous volume of information received each week from all sources. Looking for consistency? The CDN's *very first* pricing analyst (in 1963) is one of the owners—and still pricing!

Lowest Cost & Best Service...

Price is important—especially these days. Subscribers to the CDN receive 75 issues for their yearly $98; that's a little more than a dollar per valuable issue. *Bluesheet* subscribers receive 51 weekly issues plus all of the Supplemental charts for only $117 annually — and receive for free the Asksheet prices that previously cost $45! You can save the cost of an entire year's subscription on your first purchase or sale — why risk making an uninformed decision in this volatile market?

Reliability is Critical...

The CDN began publication in 1963; we continues to provide our subscribers with market information that is reliable, accurate, independent & timely. Imagine, **timely delivery every week for nearly four decades.** This is certainly a record by any standard, and one that we intend to keep intact. Any price you get elsewhere will be less than you deserve — even when their pricing sections are based on our CDN prices, they will still be weeks out of date before they begin to even think of publishing! Anything less is of little use to participants in the market who need to keep pace with ever-changing prices.

If Your Local Dealer Can't Be Without His *CDN family*, **How Can You?**

Take a look around! You will find that every dealer refers to our family of publications — as they have for over thirty-eight years!

Dedicated. Responsive. Proven.

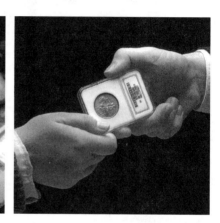

There are reasons why more collectors and dealers look to NGC first for grading their coins.

We're dedicated. Whether it's through our top expert grading team, comprehensive grading guarantee, or hobby support, NGC's dedication to numismatics is unmatched.

We're responsive. Whether you call and experience the helpful, knowledgeable support of our leading customer service reps, or take advantage of our comprehensive services from varieties and errors, to grading tiers for all budgets and timetables, NGC's responsiveness to the hobby's needs is unmatched.

We're proven. For over 12 years we've proven our commitment to integrity, impartiality, grading consistency and the betterment of the hobby. We've been there for you in years past, we're here to help you today, and we'll be there for you tomorrow.

Dedicated. Responsive. Proven. The more choices you have in grading services, the more important it becomes that you can trust your choice. That's NGC.

About the Author

David W. Lange is Director of Research for Numismatic Guaranty Corporation in Parsippany, New Jersey. His responsibilities for NGC include variety attribution, authentication, numismatic research and writing and also the preparation of customized coin presentations called PHOTO PROOFs.

In addition to the present volume, Lange is the author of companion books on Lincoln Cents and Mercury Dimes. He has also written hundreds of feature articles on United States coins and has appeared on a number of radio and television shows. His column, "From

One to Seventy," appears monthly in *The Numismatist*. He is also a frequent instructor at the American Numismatic Association's annual Summer Conference.

A lifelong collector of coins, David W. Lange was born in San Francisco in 1958. His current interests in numismatics include the coins and notes of The Philippines under United States sovereignty, as well as the modern coinage of Great Britain. He is also an avid collector of both current and obsolete coin albums.